How to Create, Sustain and Accelerate SME growth in Africa

SMALL BUSINESS BIBLE

HOW TO CREATE, SUSTAIN AND ACCELERATE SME GROWTH IN AFRICA

TARSICIUS EDEM DORPENYO

How to Create, Sustain and Accelerate SME growth in Africa

SMALL BUSINESS BIBLE

Copyright© Tarsicius Edem Dorpenyo 2018

All Rights Reserved

No part of this book may be reproduced in any form, by photocopying or by any electronic or mechanical means, including information storage or retrieval systems, without permission in writing from both the copyright owner and the publisher of this book.

Cover Design by:
Sylla Mohammed (El Jay Creatives)
eljaycreatives@gmail.com
0245683810 / 0266662125

Published by:
Wise-Age Ventures
wiseage.print@gmail.com
0206513693, 0249544508

I dedicate this book to all entrepreneurs in Africa.

KEEP GOING!

ACKNOWLEDGMENT

It is worth noting that, this book has come into being through the relentless efforts of a number of people whose contributions deserve commendation. Firstly, I would like to thank the thought leaders who agreed to share their invaluable insights on the Business Lens TV Show from which this book is couched: Captain Budu Koomson rtd., Mrs. Joyce Boakye, Mr. Ekow Mensah, Dr. Irene Egyir, Mr. Derrydean Dadzie, Ms. Fafa Doegah, Mr. Bernard Kelvin Clive, Mr. Princewill Omorguiwa and Mr. Todd Holcombe. Secondly, I thank my business partners who have supported this project in diverse ways: Ms. Josephine Fafa Doegah, General Manager of Empower Office Suites; Mr. Paul Frimpong, CEO of Westlion and Mr. Victor Kpatah, CEO of Thy Hand Video Production. This project is a true reflection of your self-abnegation and foresight.

Thirdly, it is worth noting that Ms. Abigail Esinam Adukpo, who edited and proofread this work, did an incredible job and was extremely professional in the delivery of her service.

Let me at this juncture acknowledge the contributions of my family: my father, Mr. Francis Kudjoe Dorpenyo; my mother, Madam Juana Ama Afiadenyo; my brother, Dr. Isidore Kafui Dorpenyo and his wife, Mrs. Naomi Dorpenyo; my lovely sister, Ms. Irene Sena Dorpenyo; my uncle, Mr. Alfred Tordzro and his wife, Mrs. Victoria Tordzro; my cousins: Rev.

Fr. Paul Tordzro, Ms. Eunice Tordzro, Mr. Peter Tordzro, Mr. John Tordzro, Ms. Georgina Mensah and their spouses. Thank you for your undying support, care and love.

Last but not least, thank you, dear reader for spending your hard-earned money and hard-pressed time to buy and read my book. It is my hope that you get greater value in return than you paid for. Cheers!

The author
Tarsicius Edem Dorpenyo
Chief Executive Officer,
TED Media Group.

CONTENTS

Copyright	I
Dedication	II
Acknowledgment	III
Contents	V
Introduction	VII

PART I

CHAPTER 1	**6**
The Startup Ecosystem	6
CHAPTER 2	**13**
Effective business planning strategies	13
CHAPTER 3	**26**
Co working for small businesses	26
CHAPTER 4	**32**
Agriculture entrepreneurship	32

PART II

CHAPTER 5	**39**
Digital marketing for small businesses	39

CHAPTER 6 — **50**

Branding for SMEs, Startups and their founders — **50**

CHAPTER 7 — **57**

Technology as a catalyst for business growth — **57**

CHAPTER 8

Why businesses fail often in Africa — 69

INTRODUCTION

The disproportionate growth of Small-Medium Enterprises (SMEs) in Africa shows that, the challenges facing SMEs on the continent are not entirely restricted to financing. As a developing market, most African countries lack the institutional frameworks that assist, guide and help startups and Small-Medium Enterprises (SMEs) and even mature businesses to navigate the several economic challenges that threaten their growth and survival. The Global Entrepreneurship Monitor (GEM) 2015 report identifies lack of education, inadequate market research and limited access to funds as the main causes of the termination of several rather brilliant businesses in Sub-Saharan Africa. What if we could provide entrepreneurs and their businesses knowledge on the issues that matter regarding how to start up and grow a business? A lot more businesses would survive long enough to provide employment for the growing youthful population, there will be an increase in GDP across the continent coupled with variant socio-political advantages that would accrue to the people of Africa.

Small Business Bible is a book written for Small-Medium Enterprises (SMEs). It features entrepreneurs, business analysts, financial experts, investors and educationists who provide answers to the questions that entrepreneurs find hard to answer concerning how to start, nurture, grow a business and become profitable in the process. Areas of discourse in this book have been strategically selected by a team of experts to address the challenges faced by entrepreneurs across different sectors of the economy. Some of the key issues addressed by the distinguished guests include digital marketing techniques, branding, business planning, new idea development and co working office space for small businesses.

The book is in three parts. The first part focuses on how to create a business with emphasis on idea development, business planning, co-working space and agricultural entrepreneurship.

The second part deals with how to scale your business through digital marketing, effective branding and the deployment of appropriate technology tools to enhance efficiency.

The third part focuses on why businesses fail often and what can be done to sustain home-grown businesses.

It is my fervent hope that this book assists my fellow ambitious entrepreneurs with knowledge that will help them develop globally competitive businesses to create wealth and prosperity.

How to Create, Sustain and Accelerate SME growth in Africa

PART I — BUILD

CHAPTER 1
IDEA DEVELOPMENT

Todd Holcombe - Senior faculty; Meltwater Entrepreneurial School of Technology (MEST)
Todd is a Seasoned IT executive, who brings a unique mixture of knowledge that encompasses infrastructure solutions, database / application solutions (mainframe, midrange and desktop platforms) and internet/intranet solutions.

He spent 25 years working for the bank of America where he rose through the ranks to the position of Senior Technology Manager of the Bank. He is a highly adaptable and result driven change agent.

Todd is known for being a quick study with a track record of producing results across a wide range of disciplines and in multiple industry sectors in Fortune 100 settings. He has strong ability to influence internal initiatives through highly refined organization change management techniques, structured workshop/facilitation skills and world class thought leadership.

Todd is a Senior Faculty at the Meltwater Entrepreneurial School of Technology in West Africa. Where he supervises entrepreneurs and provides advisory services to help them refine their ideas to achieve desired results.
Credit: **LinkedIn**

HOW THE MELTWATER ENTREPRENEURIAL SCHOOL OF TECHNOLOGY (MEST) GROOMS ENTREPRENEURS.

The Meltwater Entrepreneurial School of Technology recruits entrepreneurs from Nigeria, Kenya, South Africa and Cote D'Ivoire. We don't have a quota. We just look for qualified candidates who have that entrepreneurial spirit and fire in the eye that makes you feel that you truly want to be an entrepreneur. Entrepreneurship is not an easy journey so you have to look for resilience, innovative thinking and some history to see what the entrepreneurs have done to exemplify the aforementioned traits.

Before picking a trainee we want to know that you are plugged in with what is going on. What applications do you use on your phone? What are the up-and-coming trends that you have noticed and think are important? We also ask questions like "what is the best thing about you?" and "what is the worst thing about you?" These questions help us to know how introspective our prospective recruits are because, one thing about being an entrepreneur is that, it is a difficult path and you are probably going to fail and so you have to be very resilient. You have to have a lot of courage and this is not a twelve-month, one-year or two-year program. This is a path that lasts a lifetime. So we will want to know about the persons inside out. Some of the things we ask are "who is your best friend?" and "if we asked him/her to tell us about you what will he/she say?"

In a practical way we teach three disciplines: business, communications and technology. MEST is built around the premise of solving problems through technology; because technology is the most resource-friendly way to solve problems. A guy can sit down with a laptop and create Facebook. It is also a human resource friendly way of creating a lot of wealth but you have to learn to build a business because technology alone is not going to bring you jobs. Hence, you need to know a business plan, how to monetize, what your market looks like, your target market, where you sit in the market, who your competitors are. How do you differentiate and how do you put these things together into a pitch and sell your passion to investors in order to build your dream business and scale it up? It is essential that you know how to communicate not only in a pitch but in emails, interviews and with your audience. Are you talking to a CEO or to a developer? The mode of discourse will vary depending on who your audience is; hence we teach communication skills as part of our curriculum.

One of the things we teach under communications is team building. You need to find a team of three or four people who have complementary skills and not because they like each other or because they think the same. In fact, we discourage that because, friction causes heat and a lot of good ideas come out of the friction of ideas. You don't want everybody thinking alike, you want to build a company from people who are passionate about a common idea but they don't come at it from the same perspective. Putting a team together because they are your friends is not a good thing to do. We tell our teams all the time, that don't build a team because you get along socially.

When building a team pick people that aren't necessarily going to agree on everything; because a lot of innovation comes from the respect for dialogue.

INCUBATION

When we talk about innovation hubs and business incubators, it is about taking in teams that have innovative ideas or taking individuals and building them into teams to form ideas and then helping them grow. We partner with different companies and Kosmos Energy is one of them. They are an energy company; but together we created the Kosmos Innovation Centre (KIC), and they have for the past years centered on agro-tech solutions. We give them a room in our incubator at MEST and they use that to scale up their business. If you go to these competitions around Ghana (and I usually sit on many of these panels as a judge of these competitions), MEST alumni usually come up in the top three because they are more mature by the time they come into these competitions.

If you are looking to integrating our model in an educational institution like the University of Ghana for instance, one of the things to note is that we teach in a very practical way. This is not the learn-replicate-to-pass-a-test model. We teach and then you create something out of what you have learnt. All three disciplines are integrated to the greatest extent as possible and are all synchronized as you progress throughout the various stages. We do not teach anything we do not create. If we teach you java you create a java program, you maintain it and make it work. When we are teaching you android, you create a mobile application. We start out at the beginning with technology and in a very simple way. You learn scripting languages such as {html} and {css}. As part of your course you create a website for your online profiles and also get into more of backend programming after that. This is to ensure that your online profile will have server pages where it will be pulling information from. Afterwards, we start android courses where you create a mobile application for your online profile. You are to make the app fit into your screen and let it revolve around, as it should, on a mobile device and on different platforms. While the training is in progress we help you to synchronize the business deliverables and communications.

It is hard to institutionalize something like this on a large scale but what I have realized is that at the Kwame Nkrumah University of Science and Technology (KNUST), they have a branch of technology that has an entrepreneurial track where people sign up and undertake projects. It may not be part of an actual curriculum but it is run like a chess club for the entrepreneurs, where people come together and undertake projects.
What I have seen which is very surprising is that, we have computer science graduates coming to MEST who have never actually programed a java program before. They could pass their tests because they knew what the method was and they knew the syntax but they never actually created a java program. One of the things that they appreciate and which attracts them when we recruit is that they understand that we teach in a practical way so when they come through, they know that after they come out of the twelve-month curriculum, they are going to actually be able to do something.

IDEA DEVELOPMENT

When it comes to developing ideas that will be sustainable in the market, what I tell my students is: go out and find something that is a real problem, that is where the idea starts. We can all attest to the fact that there are several challenges around us; hence, there are numerous business opportunities in Ghana and Africa at large. I visited the Registrar General's office, sat there for half an hour and I can give you thirty new ideas. The point is, go, find a problem, make assumptions and validate with the right people who admit that indeed the problem is affecting their lives and then come up with a solution and validate your solutions. Once you are done, start to work on that problem and the solution that you have chosen and keep it focused.

Don't try to boil the ocean, get something that is very succinct, clear and very specific. Work on that problem and get it out soon in front of your audience, your typical client, the paying customer and see how they use it. It is very important to see quickly how the customers use your product and then start to develop it. Maybe your customers will use the product in a very different way from how you anticipated. So you learn from your customer and pivot to develop a product that customers want. One of our teams created a hand cream but when they put it out on the market after a year, the sales figures kept falling and rising in an irregular manner and they didn't know why. Little did they know that their product was an excellent mosquito repellant and was being used for that purpose instead of being the hand cream it was intended to be.

They repackaged their product as a mosquito repellant and it is one of the best products on the market. It is extremely important to put the proper mechanisms in place to collect data. Your Key Performance Indicators (KPIs) should be in place to know how your users are using your product. You always learn from your customers. Look at how the sales trends are going and pivot to make your idea work. People come up to me all the time when I am out in Osu and other places in the ecosystem with new ideas. Even my son is continually telling me about ideas and I say ideas are easy to conceive. It is doing something about them that is the hard part, so you have got to do the heavy lifting. Also we really have to get investors out there to come here and interact with the local startups. We have more mature ecosystems in areas like Nairobi, Lagos and Cape Town. Accra is developing, but investors still don't look at Ghana as a place with real Return On Investment (ROI), they think of it more as a form of donation. This is a theory of mine and I think it is a bit cultural. I think there are some great entrepreneurial successes here in Ghana but culturally you are told to keep your head down, keep working, don't talk about the money you are making and don't talk about your success; and that is not what we need. We need people celebrating their successes so that people understand that there are success stories here and that you can come and invest in some real companies that make some real money.

When we started, we were a school and then we realized that having no place for our graduates to land and having no one to help them wasn't going to work so we started the incubator. After a while we realized that we are incubating them but we are not getting the investment opportunities, so we started using Meltwater as a network tool to get the word out and we got invited to Harvard and Boston college and MIT so that these local startup companies can go there and get some investors to talk to and come back here and let the investors follow them. One of the reasons we expanded to the different countries too was not only to create that Pan Africa market for our companies to access, but also to leverage the more mature ecosystems because that is where the investors are. There certainly are a lot more investors in Lagos and Nairobi than in Accra. The incubators in Ghana are a lot less mature and once our twenty seven companies all grow and the incubators also mature, we will begin to attract a lot more investors into the country.

The first thing that struck me after being here in Ghana for a while was that you can't throw a rock without hitting an entrepreneur, everybody is an entrepreneur. People put containers in front of their houses and they run provision shops. Ghanaians have an entrepreneurial spirit imbedded in them, everybody has got the side hustles going on, everybody is doing two or three or four things. I once went to Kokrobite where we were taking surfing lessons. There was this little boy who grabbed a fence plank and whiles watching the surf lessons, he was trying to replicate what we were doing, that was day 1. On day 2 there were 3 or 4 other kids and he was teaching them how to surf. I think Ghana is a fertile environment for entrepreneurship however, we must do more.

At MEST, we stress creating globally competitive companies. When we bring entrepreneurs in as part of our recruitments we tell them: "once you cross the gate into MEST you are in an international territory, you are not in Ghana, Ivory Coast or Nigeria anymore. Ghana time does not apply here, you have to be on time, you have to be professional and you have to eschew complacency." More often than not, when companies get to a certain threshold, they get comfortable. When the founders get a house and a car, they say to themselves "it is ok for me". In business like in swimming, you either move or you sink. So you have to keep progressing and thinking long term. You should constantly be building and innovating. Constantly find out how to deepen your relationship with your customers, acquire new customers and improve on your products by redesigning and adding new features, you need to be building.

I am very bullish about the future of entrepreneurship in Ghana. When I got here about 2 years ago, when we interviewed these students who had come out of a four-year degree program I asked them: "do you have the support of your family?" I got about 50 % saying yes and 50% saying not really because "I got out of a four-year program and now they want me to go and work in a bank or be an accountant or follow that track". Now it's not so much, parents' understand that in order to really solve the unemployment problem here in Ghana and to really bring jobs and wealth back here, there has to be SMEs and that is going to start with the entrepreneurs and this is very important for the socio-economic growth of the country.

At MEST, we believe that talent is universal but access is not, so we are trying to bring access to the people who are talented but lack the opportunity to achieve great heights.

CHAPTER 2.
EFFECTIVE BUSINESS PLANNING STRATEGIES

Ekow Mensah, Management consultant

Ekow Mensah is an entrepreneurship, leadership & youth empowerment activist, an innovator, a life & personal development coach and inspirational speaker, who through his networks, has secured many speaking engagements and is well respected as an emerging global leader in Entrepreneurship, Leadership and Empowerment.

Named amongst the 50 Most Influential Under 40 Individuals in Ghana, Ekow Mensah is a serial entrepreneur who has developed a wealth of knowledge and experience in the MSME market, both as a practitioner and a multiple business owner. His responsibilities are far reaching and encompass public speaking, business consultancy, mentoring, training, coaching as well as informing policy within strategic organisations that are involved in the evolvement of entrepreneurial development, as a key contributor to economic growth. Ekow is not limited to Ghana or the continent of Africa, his work and professional alliances extend to partnerships with UK and USA based associates who together create solutions for MSMEs in accessing global markets.

Ekow is the Chairman of the Ekow Mensah Group with 5 Subsidiaries namely IConceptsPR, York Construction & Investments, Trade hub

Limited, Privateline Studios and EMANDA Global. The Ekow Mensah Group has investments in Multimedia, Construction, Retail, Finance, Education and IT and is headquartered in Ghana.

Ekow is the Founder & currently the CEO of The African Network Of Entrepreneurs (TANOE), TANOE holds a membership of about 1750 entrepreneurs across Africa primarily in Ghana, Nigeria, South Africa, Uganda, Liberia, Kenya and Zambia.

Ekow is the Founder & CEO of Impact Hub Africa, a social enterprise with flagship projects such as Marriage Support Network Africa and Speakers' Bureau.

As an Independent Consultant & Facilitator with the British Council Ghana, Ekow is engaged annually in the training and mentoring of over 3000 graduates and out of school youth in entrepreneurship, career development, IT and leadership throughout Ghana.

As a personal development & life coach, Ekow coaches individuals and organizations globally on leadership development, career advancement, performance maximization, skills enhancement and start-up and entrepreneurship development.

Credit: ekowmensah.com/aboutem

My encounters with startups in Ghana have been very exciting. A lot of the startup entrepreneurs are very passionate and most of them have a relentless belief and optimism in their ideas and the businesses they want to run and that is honestly a plus. Unfortunately though, this optimism prevents them from seeing the reality of the pitfalls, so they end up putting so much energy, time and money in building their ventures, majority of which fail in the long run due to a number of challenges.

Firstly, most of these startups in Ghana and Africa, at large, are not innovative in their business endeavours. They look around, see what someone has done and then say to themselves; "okay, this idea works and people are making a lot of money with it", and they just want to replicate it without adding value. Also, sometimes they are not able to identify their target market and they are not able to package their products to attract customers in the target markets. Furthermore, they don't open up for partnerships, they want to do everything by themselves. They want to be known as the CEO/ founder and so eventually they remain small, so, yes there are a lot of very passionate people out there but they are very small and doing small things and eventually when the competition sets in with people who have the money and resources, they are blown out of the market.

Entrepreneurship has always been with us. Our people have always loved running their own businesses. In recent years, entrepreneurship has been repackaged in such a way that it is considered a prestige and social status symbol to own a business, hence everybody wants to have a business. I tell young graduates all the time; entrepreneurship is not necessarily about having your own business but it is about being resourceful and skillful enough to contribute to a business whether someone else's or yours. However, because the philosophy has always been "I want to have my own business to elevate my value and the way people see me", a lot of people want to start their own businesses. The whole philosophy of entrepreneurship has been wrongly perceived.

There is this notion that we have a lot of accidental entrepreneurs, thus when students are out of school and there is no job for them they start something on their own. It is true and I don't just encounter people like that, I actually advocate for that. I tell people that the best way to get a job is to start something. You could send your CV to various companies but with the same effort you put in distributing your CV, you can actually find a product and still sell it to these companies. The difference between the first one, sending your CV and the other, selling your products and services, is that, you are putting in a lot of energy but the perception is different. When you sell a product or service to a company and you are able to market it to them, they identify your skills from the way you present your products and services. They will look at you as somebody who will best fit into their business. Therefore, when there is an opportunity to employ they would want to bring you onboard. Also, there are a lot of people who, for the lack of employment, end up doing something on their own and then eventually they realize that what they are doing is doing well so they reposition themselves and get into that business full time. So quite a number of entrepreneurs did not intend to be entrepreneurs but why should they sit home instead of going out and doing something and being useful to themselves?

FUNDAMENTALS OF THE BUSINESS PLAN

Writing a business plan is daunting because it is a specialized document. It is comparable to building a house. If you have money to build a house you can go to an architect to sketch your house, then you show it to a foreman or a contractor and he/she will be able to actualize it for you. However, if you want to build a house that will stand the test of time, you need to go through the process of getting an architect, checking suitability, then you get a civil engineer and go through the process till you get to the point where your house is built and you are sure this will stand the test of time. It is the same for business plans.

I think anyone who wants to build a business that will stand the test of time and that will outlive him/her needs to commit to putting together a business plan, because building a business is not just a nine-day wonder. It is something that you have to carefully and intentionally be committed to working on. Of course, there are experts who can help you to make it a solid document but then as a person you can go through the process of writing a business plan and it shouldn't scare anybody. This is your business. No one will know your business better than you do especially when you dream something that is original or something that is innovative. Nobody can write a business plan for you without your input, so when you start from the point where you believe that nobody can understand your business more than you do, then, you start putting together your plans. I never scare my students or the people I consult for about business plans. I try to tell young entrepreneurs that, the business plan is a document which they themselves are the best people to write.

You start your business plan with the end in mind. How would your business look when it is successful? You just have to dream it and once you are thinking about it put the points down. How would it look like when your business is successful? How many employees will it have? How will the management look like? What location will you be in? What will the services and products look like? What kind of PR will you put in, what kind of marketing and what would your sales look like? So in answering those questions you put them together into what we call the executive summary. Note however that the executive summary is what is written last because it is the summary of all the various aspects of the business, all the elements of the business plan. You put them together and have it placed at the beginning of the plan. Anybody who is out there, if your profession is not writing a business plan, don't worry too much, start with the end in mind, how will your business look like when it is successful? Have a projection of maybe five years to ten years, those are the timelines. Tell me that maybe according to your projections your business will be successful in the next ten years, so start with that in mind and then write.

The first thing you write is the description of this business so, you talk about it in your executive summary. What kind of business is this, and what kind of industry is it going to play in and to what kind of sector do you belong? Where are the associations and the networks that this business falls in? These are the things you consider, so at that point you are not even talking about the product or the solution, you are just giving the overview of the business. You can't just write this part just by sitting down, you will have to do a bit of research.

If you want to go into dressmaking for instance, you know it is in the fashion industry. What is the analysis of the fashion industry? What is the worth of the fashion industry? What are the trends in the fashion industry? And what are the policies that govern the fashion industry? So to finish the description of the industry you must do a research of the industry that you are looking at. At this stage you are looking at why the business you want to do is important and which sector it is going to go into and which industry because the industry is bigger than the sector. Afterwards, you put all the narrative about the business together into what we call the Business Description. In reality, it shouldn't be difficult but of course there are some jargons and words and phrases that you have to add to make it look professional, but it is an organic document and what I mean by that is that, it is a growing document, you don't just write it like a Bible or Quran. It is something that evolves, it has to be something that guides you so basically that is the first step.

When you are done with the description then you come to the product and services or solution that you are bringing to the market, because every business addresses certain problems and challenges in the marketplace and the various elements of a business plan differ depending on who is reading it. The generic one is what we call product and services or solutions. What solutions are you bringing to the marketplace? Out of the description you will be able to determine how you are going to package your product, who you are going to sell it to and how the product looks like. That's where you are actually going to describe your product and service. You will have to determine the target market segment you want because you know the product and service better and you know what key problems it addresses or what target market your product seeks to meet. If I take your business plan and read it, I should know for instance, that you are making your product for babies hence I will know what alkaline component etc. that the product should have. It all depends on your target market. In your absence if someone picks your business plan he/she should be able to know what the components of the product are and how you are packaging it, and how you will deliver your product to your customers. Who will do the delivery and where will customers find your product for purchase? I think it is the best place to put your unique selling proposition and your value proposition: what is different about this water that you want to sell?

Once you are done with the products and services the next thing to consider is how you are going to market it. You have to think about that and that is when your marketing sales and promotions come in. Once your products and services are properly outlined then you look at the market: who you are going to sell to, and that is one of the challenges that we face. We think that once you are coming up with a product and service that is so amazing, it has to be for everyone. Trust me; there is no product in the world now that is for everyone, every product has a target market.

A product might fit for another use but it doesn't mean that is the target market. When you look at all the banks that we have, in fact, we have over thirty five commercial banks in Ghana. Even though anybody can go to a bank and open a bank account, the bank, through its market analysis knows the kind of clients that it is looking for. With this book - Small Business Bible, the fact that it is out on the market does not mean that it is for everybody. It is targeted at business owners, graduates, policy makers and investors. If you go to Movenpick Ambassador Hotel located in Accra, it is a hotel just like any other hotel, but even its number of stars will determine who their target is. So in your business plan as an entrepreneur, you have to be very careful when it comes to your market analysis, don't be too broad. As much as possible, narrow it down to that one person who you think is a best fit when it comes to your target market.

I think the biggest challenge with entrepreneurs is that we are told to dream big and in the process we tend to think you will have to target everybody in the market, but that is not possible. If you are producing water for instance, everybody drinks water but kids cannot buy it so then, even though water is for everybody, the people that buy are the people that you are looking for, so the kid's mom and dad should be your target market. Even when you produce diapers the target market is the baby's mother, even though the baby is the user. So that is where the challenge is. During marketing analysis, people are not able to tell the difference between users and the target market: those with the purchasing power, because in some cases, the people who actually use the product are not those who buy them. When bringing a product into the market, you have to go into analyzing who the users are: the paying market.

When we were growing up we knew about day care centers. Now they call them Montessori, and the name itself defines the target market you are looking for. So even though the users of the nursery are the kids they are not the ones that are paying. On their advertising flyers, you see babies sitting down and being happy and learning but they are not doing those adverts or promotions for the babies. They are doing them for the people who can afford, that is their parents and their guardians so that is one of the things to look at when you are doing marketing analysis.

When you are done with that, you have to look at your competition. I have met startup owners who say I don't have a competition. This is because in their minds what they are doing is unique and nobody is doing it already, but the fact is this: every product or every service has a competition. Even in cases where your product doesn't have a replica in the market, you need to know that there are complementary products and there are the things that can be used in place of your product. When Facebook started it wasn't the only social media platform at the time. We had Myspace and other platforms.

I am sure in their business plan they identified who their competitor was. You have to actually write out your top five competitors and in planning, you have to do a bit of research to find out who your competitors are, what they are doing, where they are doing it, what their plans and strategies are and how you, with whatever resources you have, can either beat them or present your solution in such a way that people will be able to compare and choose your product over that of your competitors. So competition analysis is a very big point in business planning and it is one of the things people should be careful about.

You need to do your analysis very well: look at your competitors, those who are doing the same things as you and those who are doing complementary products and services. In fact one of the things that is interesting is when you look at coca cola, who is their main competitor, everybody would say Pepsi but that is not true. To coca cola, their number one competition is water. Any time you are thirsty they want you to go for coke or any of their other products instead of water. They know it is a matter of choice for the consumer, hence whatever prevents you from going for coke is what their competition is. You have to look at what the main competition is and what the complementary competition is.

After you have finished with that, you have to go into what it will take to bring this product out; that is, the promotion, your marketing and your sales. For some products you have to focus on production thus, you are the manufacturer but after you have produced you will have to decide through your business plan whether you will be the same person to go out there and market it. If you are not the same person who will go out there and market it then in your marketing plan, you have to decide to build a distribution chain so that you are the manufacturer but you have distributors who are your wholesalers and they will then build your retailers. You will realize that when you go to Nestle, even though they manufacture products, they don't sell. They have their distributors, therefore they produce, give it to them and they will have their retailers. So when you need a product you don't go to Nestlé's office, you go to a distributor, a wholesaler or a retailer. All these things are to be clearly identified, and that is one of the challenges when it comes to startups - they want to do everything. I have a marketing company and you have a production company we should be partners so that you focus on your production, that is your area of expertise, and I market. When you talk about branding, promotion and sales, all those elements will be captured in your business plan at the promotion segment.

Also, you look at the people who are going to perform the duties mentioned above, your management structure. The management structure is essential especially for businesses that are going to look for money. You may have a good idea but you may not be the best candidate to run the business, therefore even though you have a good idea you may need somebody to be the head of the business because there is a difference between what makes a successful entrepreneur and a successful business manager. It is rare to have an individual who embodies entrepreneurial traits and managerial skills. Entrepreneurs, such as I, always have new ideas, and that is why most at times we don't even do a business plan. What if we do a business plan then the next day we have a new idea and we want to change? So, the moment you fashion out your business plan then, you find somebody who can run the business. However, if you are going to lead the new venture, it should be captured in your management team, that is, where you put your name and anybody who is going to help you and these people could even be people who you have not yet employed but you are going to look at , and then what kind of candidate you need for your business so that the moment you start recruiting you know who fits the job.

In addition, you need to do an analysis of what your organizational structure is going look like. This is under the operations and management segment. How are you going to run your business from start to finish? You need to capture all these details in your plan so that when you have new employees, you just take your operational plan and then you show them this is how we run this business. Due to the absence of this plan in many businesses, people are running businesses that look big but an analysis of their operations indicates that they are still one-man businesses. When you take the owners out of the business everything grinds to a halt because there are no processes, systems nor structures.

After you have figured out who is going to run the business through the management plan and how they are going to run it (which is captured in the management plan), the next salient factor to examine is the financial management plan. This is one of the things I always advise startups on. Traditionally, we are very people-centered. Most of the things we want to do, we want to do them either for free or we want to get people to test them to see if they are good. We don't start with an orientation that what we are engaged in is a business and whatever we do as long as we call it a business, the main factor that makes our venture qualify as a business is when we have somebody who is willing to buy and pay us for our products or services at a profit.

I could be selling a glass of water for ten cedis, however, if someone bought it for nine cedis, invariably, I might think I have made a profit of 1 cedi but I have forgotten that there are other expenses that have gone into bringing the product into the market for people to buy. Most new entrepreneurs don't do good analysis of their products, the cost and the expected sales revenue.

When you are preparing a financial plan, because you probably are not experienced in building a business plan, this is what I always advise on what should go into this part of the business plan. Firstly, you look at expenditure and for how much you are going to sell the product. You have to look at your expenses, or budget, what will it take to set this business up? Once you have that properly planned out, that is your expenditure. The next question is how are you going to get the money to set your business up? What kind of income are you looking at, is it through the sale of your products and services or is it through investments? If you choose to seek investment, before you meet an investor you should be able to find out what you need and what component of equity you will give in exchange for what you need. You need to look at what you need in light of what you project to spend and what your sales forecast looks like.

You have to look at your cash flow statement: your inflows and outflows, because you always need to have a working capital so that in case you are not getting business in two or three weeks, four, five, or six months, you will still be able to survive. At the end of the day you do a projection. I advise people to look at a three-year forecast of their sales, expenditure and how much they are going to make (revenue). When you take the difference between your income and expenditure, what do you have left? These are the features that the finance people look for. Furthermore you have to do a break even analysis, which is basically the point where how much you are putting in the business and how much you are getting will be are at par. Thus you are at the point where your expense and your income are the same and profit is zero. Then you can project that beyond the breakeven point: where I have already paid my expenses whatever comes will be profit. When you are starting your business, in the first year as well as the second, you might not make profit but it doesn't mean that you didn't make money. In the third year, maybe you might have made enough money to cover cost and still you have some monies left and that is when you start making profit year in and year out after tax. Whiles you do the analysis of all those things, note at this point that you are just projecting.

You come through a journey where you analyze your business. You look at what is going to go in, who is going to run it, how much it's going to sell and at the end of the day, you are doing a projection based on what you think your capacity is. At the end of the day, when you do the three-year projections and you realize that after three years you are going to have a break even, then it is likely that it's in the fourth year that you will start making profit. So when somebody puts in their money they are not going to put pressure on you to start giving them dividend from the first, second or third years. That is what you will eventually have to summarize and bring into what you call the executive summary.

Every business has the investment face where you keep putting in money to the point where you have put in enough and then you are getting enough; back such that what you are getting equals what you put in. By research, if a business survives beyond three years, the likelihood that it is going to survive is high because we have realized that about 90% of all startups collapse in the first three years because that is when most people don't get their projections right.

Some people are very optimistic, they make fabulous projections but I always advise that you develop a prototype first before you make projections. The prototype stage is when you actually develop the product you intend to sell, go to the market and have it tested by the market. The best business plans are the ones that come from businesses that have already prototyped. This is because you are able to tell from the experience gathered during your months of prototyping how the people accept the product and how much they are willing to buy it. If you spend X amount of money to sell Y number of products, you can then project that if you get Z amount of money you can get K amount of profit. It becomes a fallacy when you just do projections in your mind knowing you haven't even sold one product. There are people who have not sold even one product yet they have extreme projections.

CONCLUSION

We struggle as a people to build companies that grow to multinational status. There are a lot of factors that contribute to this phenomenon, and I don't think that largely it's our fault. The first thing I will look at is our orientation and the educational system. The system doesn't enable us to think big. We are always in survival mode. We look for the little that we can get to survive and that stifles innovative thinking. Somebody starts a business, gets the first one hundred thousand Ghana cedis and she/he thinks he/she is rich because they can buy a car and get a decent accommodation.

Also, we fantasize a lot but we don't dream. When you dream you actually start putting together goals, targets and timelines, but when you fantasize you think by sitting down, everything is possible. Our religious orientation also affects our psyche and understanding of business processes. When we go to church (which majority of us do), we are made to believe that everything is possible so then we don't do the necessary planning and hard work that leads to success. We need to start building networks and partnerships to promote growth.

In addition, I think the enabling environment is also missing. The ecosystem is still young and there aren't a lot of success stories of people that have been able to build global businesses. As a result we are not able to read and get inspiration from their success, and also get mentored on how businesses are built. Most of the stories, I am sure, you and I have read are stories of people outside Africa and you know that the setting is different. Also, there are government policies that prevent us from being able to succeed most of the time.

I think in addition to the above, we lack the knowledge to be able to build global businesses and that is something that has to do with capacity building and the commitment to be able to go through what it takes to build a global business, so I will say the orientation is the problem.

Lastly, we lack the needed investment to be able to be audacious. Our market is small - Ghana's population is just about twenty five million people and out of that number I don't believe even 50 % of us have the purchasing power. If you want to build global businesses, it is not just about staying local but being able to build something local that can go global. Therefore, when you are building a product or service it is not just a solution for Ghana but it has to be a solution that transcends the country.

There are a lot of factors, but I will still go back to the mindset. We don't have the knowledge, the technical know-how to build those companies that can go global, we just get excited about little successes.

CHAPTER 3

CO-WORKING FOR SMALL BUSINESSES

Josephine Fafa Doegah, General Manager-Empower office suites

Her dynamic and revolving career of over 15years reflects excellent sales, organisational, customer service skills, as well as several transferable skills to deliver outstanding results in any corporate environment. These combined skills have given her the ability to quickly understand complex concepts, identify and solve problems, turn ideas into logical strategies, and implement systems that optimize productivity and customer satisfaction. Exceptional ability to identify and resolve problems in timely manner, proven ability to build productive teams that deliver exceptional client service and the unique ability to identify and implement cost saving measures are also attributes She possesses.

Formerly she was the Area Manager –Regus Accra where her responsibilities span from recruiting, inducting, training and developing centre team to maximise their performance and engagement.

Getting a business space in busy cities across Africa can be draining, not only in terms of energy you put in the search but also on your pocket as a business owner. Small business owners across Africa face the peculiar challenge of getting office spaces fit for business activities at locations that are easily accessible by clients. As a result, most entrepreneurs are working from their homes, from coffee shops and other places which were not designed for office activities. The main difficulty entrepreneurs have regarding office space is the location and its accompanying cost.

Every startup has some sort of capital which it uses to start the business known as the startup capital. It is not prudent to lock up your capital in renting an office space irrespective of how necessary that need is to the success of your businesses. It is also the case that most landlords in Ghana demand the payment of at least two years in rent advance before leasing out their facilities to tenants. As a result of these challenges, new businesses avoid such arrangements and resort to working from obscure locations with conditions considered to be inappropriate for business activities.

Getting an office in the Central Business District costs a lot of money due to the high demand for such facilities by multinationals and firms with deep pockets. Central Business Districts are home to most head offices, government departments and ministries, hence there is a stiffer competition for facilities in these areas. For startups and Small to Medium scale Enterprises (SMEs), it is not necessary for them to compete with big firms for office space in the Central Business Districts because, they can have access to their clients even from remote locations. With the advent of technology there are so many ways of getting in touch with your clients such as emails, social media and different ways to make yourself accessible to your clients. Apart from the cost of renting spaces in the Central Business District, there are issues regarding monthly utility bills, administrative expenses, internet expenses and other related costs that come with owning an office which make it very difficult for new businesses to maintain functional office spaces.

NEW BUSINESS MODELS

There are new opportunities coming up to assist new businesses maintain decent offices for their employees. One such opportunity is premised on the philosophy of sharing, rather than owning. The sharing economy which has transformed the transportation and hospitality industries with the introduction of UBER and AirB&B respectively is gaining grounds in the office renting business. The model is known as the shared office model. With the shared office model, a whole floor is managed by a renting company which takes care of cleaning, provision of utility, internet, furniture etc. and rents the rooms or desks in the rooms out to businesses on a short term or long term basis. The spaces are rented on an hourly, daily, weekly, monthly or even on yearly basis depending on the need and resources of the customer. There are different types of arrangement under the shared office model.

There are co-working spaces, where a tenant shares an office with workers from other companies. A company may rent just a desk in a room for a worker hence, he/she only owns the desk space, and payment is made per number of desks used by workers of a particular company. Co-working spaces afford patrons the opportunity to meet and dialogue with people from different company backgrounds through events and also as a result of the proximity. Co-working offers tremendous opportunities in terms of networking with people from different firms. You know that you are right next to somebody whom you can network with. The networking opportunity is open right there in your face and the person next to you can be your next client and you can also engage another person's business by contracting him/her to undertake some work for you. If you are a web designer, for instance, and you have people from five different companies in your co-working office, you could easily get a deal from all five of them.

The other model is: private office. It operates in such a way that a company rents an entire room as its office on a floor yet shares amenities such as kitchen, meeting room and administrative support with other offices on the floor. Cost of utility, internet, salary of cleaners and receptionist is shared among the firms on the floor. Regarding this model, the main targets are law firms and other companies who have confidential information of clients and need a higher degree of privacy compared to others. They however, also enjoy similar benefits as the co-working space because you can meet people in the hallway, kitchen or internal events and make clients out of them. Let us not forget however, that the cost sharing is the biggest advantage with these models. You get to share the cost of utility, the internet, and the salaries for the receptionist, cleaners etc. hence, your overhead costs will be minimal, and that is the biggest reason why a lot of these people are now opting for these serviced offices.

The third model, known as the virtual office is for companies that do not need a physical office space to operate or are constantly on the move. This model gives businesses access to business address, telephone services, post office box address etc. You may not have the physical office as most companies have, however, you get to use the address of where you are registered virtually on your complementary cards and other official documents. You are not physically present but you are there "virtually" hence, the name virtual offices. If a client comes in search of a company which is signed on to the virtual package, the receptionist will take any messages and pass them on to the firm through agreed mediums. The virtual company model gives your company a representation at a very minimal cost.

The cost is relatively lower than the other models since this package does not involve physical occupancy of the facility. The virtual offices are basically for people who are on the go and do not have to be at one place to pick their phone calls and receive packages. You will have somebody who can receive them for you at the reception, you also have somebody who can pick calls for you. Also, note that you are sharing heads, hence, you don't have to pay the receptionist's salary alone, you don't have to worry about that. You can just focus on your core business, you don't have to worry about your office costs and needs.
The shared office model is becoming popular because people are

realizing that you don't need a large space for yourself to be productive. You could just have a desk to yourself and be as productive as you like. You have your desk, your laptop, internet and you are offered a phone by the operator of the shared space. With these you can be very productive. In today's business world, networking is very important and that is one of the key pull factors to these shared offices.

Firms that come into serviced offices are companies trying to find solutions that are flexible enough and tailored specifically to their needs, based on the kind of services they are rendering to their clients. They want flexibility, and with the co-working, there is a lot of flexibility in there for entrepreneurs, SMEs and freelancers who usually have a small budget. Due to their financial constraints, small business owners come in wanting to use the space for probably an hour or two or even a week and we have packages like that, which can be for short terms and cost less than you would pay if you were to rent an office space. It is not prudent to pay for a whole month and not be there always. The cardinal service that most of these people look out for is flexibility and these offices are ideal for people looking for flexibility.

CHALLENGES

With the co-working (that is the sharing of an office with different companies), you come to work in the morning. Obviously you have a desk so you just go to your desk and start to work. There are different options you can choose from: you can have a permanent desk or a flexible desk which you can hold hourly, daily, weekly or monthly as it suits your needs. But if you have a permanent desk you can come to the office on a daily basis and you will have a locker designated to you where you can keep your documents which you don't intend carrying to and fro, and you will have a key to it. You can sit at your desk, start working and you can work from 8:00 to 5:00 every day or till whenever you want, it is entirely up to you. If you are expecting guests or clients you will be informed when they come in, if you have a meeting you can book the meeting room to use at a the designated time – this is flexibility at its best.

The market for serviced offices is really ripe for investment because, this is the gap that has been identified and a lot of people are trying to fill this gap by opening up all these co-working spaces for entrepreneurs and all these people who need to keep a professional address and professional support to start up their businesses. Once a serviced office operator can give these kinds of supports to these startups and firms, then their businesses are going to kick off because there are a lot of people starting their own businesses. These days everybody wants to be an entrepreneur and it is a great opportunity for people willing to provide bespoke office services to get into the business as soon as possible because there is high demand.

The biggest challenge that entrepreneurs looking to set up their own co-working space need to consider critically is the pricing. They need to get their pricing right. If you fix your price right and your services are tailored to suit every single person and you are flexible enough to adjust to everybody's requirement, you can be profitable in no time. As I said, the pricing just depends on what your clients need. A client may come in and may not want to use the internet, he/she just needs a quiet desk to work on. That price may differ from someone who wants to use the internet. A client may want it for an hour or two or the whole day, thus the prices differ whether you want it for a day or two or a week. It also depends on the kind of facility that you are looking at. Some may have a locker, a side drawer and some may have a cabinet.

The costs for these facilities vary; hence it is the facilities you are using that determine how much you are charged. A Co-working space or shared office in Spintex in Accra will probably be cheaper that one located in the Central Business District such as the Octagon, where the Empower office suite is located. The building is top notch and the business address alone can help you sell your business offering to prospective clients. Also the administrative services, support and the professionalism will be different from one co-working space to another.

With the co-working, one of the key challenges you might face is privacy. People looking for exclusive services due to the nature of their jobs are advised to take up additional services that we may have. Maybe take a locker to keep your stuff in or you may decide to use the meeting rooms at a discount to make private calls and other activities that do not need audience or eavesdropping. So as said earlier, the watchword is flexibility. We will come up with different solutions that may help you because there is no way you can tell this client who cannot afford a private office to leave the co-working space to take a private office. So you give such a client different combinations of options that he/she can work with.

CHAPTER 4

AGRICULTURAL ENTREPRENEURSHIP

Irene S. Egyir (BSc (Agric) MPhil Ph.D (AgricEcon) (Ghana))

Dr. Irene Susana Egyir is a Senior Lecturer in the University of Ghana at Department of Agricultural Economics and Agribusiness, College of Agriculture and Consumer Sciences. She holds a Ph.D from the University of Ghana, Legon in the year 2003.

She has engaged herself in a number of consultancies such as study on the promotion of youth employment in agriculture and rural enterprise program. She has also collaborated with institutions like the Ministry of Trade and Industry, African Development Bank, RUAF From-Seed-to-Table (FStT) Impact Monitoring Plan for Accra and the International Water Management Institute. Dr. Egyir has also made a number of contributions to various book chapters. She has published a number of articles in journals, and written a number of articles in Technical reports, discussion papers and also contributed to conference proceedings.

She is the Head of Department of Agricultural Economics and Agribusiness. University of Ghana.

Dr. Egyir has founded a development NGO named Multi-Features and Capacity Enhancing Services which links urban micro-entrepreneurs to Research, Extension, Finance, Consulting and Cooperative and Media (REFCOM) Services.

credit: ug.edu.gh/aea/staff

The challenge with agriculture in Ghana is that most of the farmers are poor and the perception out there is that agriculture is the gateway to poverty. This perception is ingrained in us so much so that if you tell someone you want to be a farmer, you have in one way or the other declared that you want to be poor for the rest of your life and it makes me very sad. Agriculture is not a way to poverty at all if you look at the tilling of the land and the rearing of livestock, they started with man and that is how we have sustained ourselves for centuries. We pursued agricultural activities to feed and then it became a way of life. We went around gathering and hunting before we got to the stage where we started planting seeds and building houses. You put a seed in the soil and if God sends rains it germinates and comes out as maize, millet or rice.

For so many years now however, farming has become a business in the sense that it is considered an economic activity. Therefore you ought to organize resources, combine them in different proportions to get a desired output which you will place on the market and set a price for, so that you can get revenue out of the sales. If the revenue is good enough to cover your cost of production you earn profit and then you are in business. The profit is the incentive that drives you to continue to do what you are doing and scale it up.

In our part of the world we practise agriculture as peasants and what that means is that we are not actually targeting the market. If we want to eat sorghum, we grow sorghum, but if we have need for salt, which we don't grow, we sell part of what we grow to be able to purchase salt, or whatever we lack. However, over the years, the needs basket of farmers has grown even for those who are peasants. Children will have to pay to go to school and you need medical care, other wellbeing issues also come into play. What this means is that the farmer's mind should change from peasantry to commercial. As with many things in Africa and in most developing countries, we have realized that the speed with which we want our farmers to change their minds from just thinking of livelihood in a very narrow way to being entrepreneurial is not happening. As entrepreneurs, farmers will have to use what they know and keep learning because if you want to be an entrepreneur, you ought to be a learning organization. You can only learn so that your decisions will be based on soundness and that is where we have not reached yet. So you see, our farmers are still using old practices or even when they have been introduced to improved practices, they don't want to invest in that and therefore they go back and forth. If you don't get good yield, you may not be able to sustain yourself in the market because if you sell just a little, you will plough back just a little and you will continue to stay at that little space and that is where poverty comes in.

INSTITUTIONS

It is true that we have institutions that are set up to train practitioners of the agriculture sector however, they have not lived up to the billing. When we talk about institutions, I will go back to theory. The institutions are operating as public, private or voluntary organizations. With public agricultural institutions, you are talking about the Ministries, Departments and Agencies (MDAs) and they are at the national level, regional level and district level. Their main job is to formulate policies and see to it that they are being implemented and do monitoring and evaluations and also facilitate the environment for agriculture. It is for this reason that government is providing some infrastructure to be able to set the environment right. In Ghana, you would realize that after independence, the state took it upon itself to be in agriculture. State farms were engaged in production and all value addition in the agro processing industries. Every region had something relating to agriculture and the state was in charge of these facilities.

Then after the 1970s the policies switched and maybe even from the second republic coming down, the private sector was expected to take over fully from the state. For some reasons the private sector is still yet to take over because although we say that the farmers are in the private sector, because they are not businessmen/women they are not thinking business-like. We still think that they are out of the business economy, hence the few who are operating as businesses in the private sector can be counted. If you go into oil palm, there are lots of oil palm plantations, same with banana plantations, however just two or three firms own them all. If you go into the pineapple and the nontraditional export commodities, there we can identify some commercial farms. If you go into maize cultivation which is the main food of our country, you can count just a few large scale automated farms, the rest are in the hands of the peasants. Talking about other grains, rice is coming up gradually and we are having some commercial farms because now we have the Ghana

Commercial Agricultural Project (GCAP) that is supporting some farms. We call them: the nucleus farmers, to hold hands with small scale farmers called out-growers to do something that is more commercially-oriented. However, if you take cocoa, our major cash crop, the production is not being done in that vigorous manner accompanied by planned business models, and our farmers are not aggressive in their quest to increase production to earn more money.

That kind of business orientation is still not there. There are commercial plants such as rubber, which are purely nonfood and you would expect that their farmers would be more commercially oriented but they are not. They still do not see it as a business where they will say let us change our mindset and be businessmen; you know businessmen fight the risks in the industry to gain the profit they desire.

CREDIT FACILITIES

In the late 90s we had loans being given to farmers at a rate lower than what the market was willing to offer the non-agriculture sector. There were difficulties in paying back the loans and the banks that were offering these services such as the Agricultural Development Bank (ADB), Corporative Banks and even the Ghana Commercial Bank (GCB) all had some performance challenges because of payback issues. They had challenges with getting more money to give out, so what happens today is that farmers have to go to the open market to borrow. The open market for funds is from the rural banks, savings and loans companies, credit unions and then the commercial banks.

Sometimes government looks for some funds that are supposed to charge lower than the market interest rate and gives to farmers, but that model is not sustainable due to changes in government and the corresponding change in policy directions. I remember under the Millennium Development Authority (MiDA) there was a model aimed at commercializing agriculture and farmers were trained as businesses.

There was a model called farming business school where they taught farmers how to do their business plans. After the training the farmer organizations were given some loans to help them buy improved seeds, fertilizers and then also link them to markets. But individual farmers who did not join such groups found it difficult to access capital. Even those who were part of the groups, when the projects were over they somehow withdrew and that is where I also find it difficult to understand what else should be done. Although government is no longer doing state farming, the whole issue of technical advising in terms of agricultural extension officers is still free. In every district there are at least thirty agriculture agents who are trained to package good information to teach farmers as groups or as individuals.

We always say that one agriculture agent is to about five hundred farm households. If that is the case, then ICT is here to assist. The mobile phone has come to our rescue. Recently our own databases suggest that, every farm household probably has at least one mobile phone to call or send text messages to. There are literates in every farm household because we found out that there is a class six pupil who can write zero to nine and can even place a call in every farm household. Also, you don't need much literacy to operate a mobile phone. At the moment we have e-extension facilities and e-officers to assist farmers using technology. They are doing all kinds of modeling to facilitate communication with farmers. Farmers, however, still want the face-to-face interaction and are not convinced about the viability of the new media and therefore are looking for an extension officer to be present in their farms all the time before they listen.

Another missing area that we always talk about is market assess. Farmers are told to do things and if they do them they will have enough of the harvest. The question left unanswered however is who is giving the farmer a good price? After farmers toil to harvest their products, intermediaries, wholesalers or retailers who buy them do not offer good prices to the farmers and since their options are limited, the farmers are forced to sell at relatively cheaper prices than what they expect to sell them for. There are several factors that affect the prices offered these farmers and some are the road network that the intermediaries use in transporting their purchases to the market place where they will be sold. There is also the issue of the lack of storage facilities. The intermediaries who buy perishable farm produce know that by the time they move from the farm gates to the urban market, about 50% of the produce is lost to post harvest losses so, there are so many things that we are contending with. However, I believe that if you are a business person who is into farming, you will identify these as your risk areas. Farmers who are business-minded overcome these challenges. In recent times, we have had a few elite farmers who are doing well, but the majority of our farmers are still down there and we will still tag them poor as if they like it.

The last one is about the rural economy itself. Majority of farming activities that go on in our part of the world happen in the rural areas, but if the rural economy itself is not set with the good socio-economic facilities, farming cannot be done well. I teach a course called rural economy and I have realized that because we are not developing the rural economy, graduates will not go and live in the huts and walk seven miles, use hoe and cutlass and put seed in the soil and pray for rain. This is because in the University we are teaching them farming that is with strategic planning and that is why I am not surprised the agriculture graduates are looking for work in the banks and other corporate settings. The banks should also be thinking about agriculture because it shouldn't matter if my student works with the bank, if they do work with the banks they would enhance the banks' dealings with the agricultural entrepreneurs.

EDUCATION OF AGRICULTURE GRADUATES

Let's talk first and foremost about the courses offered in the higher institutions of learning. If you are an agricultural economist especially from the University of Ghana, you are an agricultural scientist. We train students in quantitative analytical skills and it is biology, chemistry, physics, mathematics, and agricultural engineering. You learn genetics, biochemistry then you come to the business aspect where you learn project analysis and farm management. You also undergo training in marketing and now we are expending more energy on teaching business planning, business policy, agrifood business, and for those who are much more concerned about the economics we do macro-economics, micro economics and econometrics as well.

By the time you complete your course from the department either as an agribusiness or an agricultural economist, you are so quantitatively-oriented that you can be placed anywhere. When you go to the farm or to services sector whether to teach, to do research, be a farm accountant, general manager etc. your skills will be adequate. You are given the principles of business and it includes administration as well therefore, our students are not taught to be exclusively farmers because, that would limit what they can do. I graduated from the Agricultural Economics department in 1990. After my graduation, I went to the farm because I wanted to understand farming. I did agriculture extension. I tried to understand the thinking of the farmer but I was not trained to be a farmer and so if one finishes school and you say he/she should start a farm business because the person knows the ingredients of farming you will be wrong.

Today, in the University of Ghana, every graduate takes entrepreneurship as a core. It doesn't matter whether you are learning history, archaeology or agriculture. The mind to start something on your own is there and a lot of my students are on the farms. I have been to Ghana Rubber Estates Limited (GREL), Benso Oil and Palm Plantation (BOPP) and all the big farms in the country and I see agriculture-trained graduates there. It is not true that agriculture-trained graduates are not interested in working in agriculture. When I finish school, and I am looking for work and the Agricultural Development Bank offers me a job or Barclays Bank takes me as a customer service representative there is nothing wrong with it.

No firm will give a 24 year old lady or gentleman money to start an agricultural venture that relies solely on rain. If there is an enclave where there is accommodation, irrigation and an older and experienced person coaching and mentoring the youth through incubations hubs more graduates will be seen starting out as agricultural entrepreneurs. Agriculture-trained graduates are ready, in fact, they are the ones in the ministries, departments and agencies but you cannot tell them to go and live in places where the accommodation is what their fathers wanted them to move away from. Even the farmers do not want their sons to do the same things they have been doing for years.

It is not that they don't want their wards to be farmers but they want them to farm using an approach different from what has been used since the Gold Coast days. I once visited a village in the Ashanti region where I met a farmer who said to me: "look at my palms, my son is in your school and I buy him things so that his palm will not be as hard as mine, we love the job but this is the reality" he said.

When you go to other developed places not many people are on the field farming because you don't need a lot of people to be farmers before you feed your people. In some places we have 5% to 10% of the people engaged in farming but due to the use of machinery and the availability of support systems and innovative thinking they are driving the growth of their economies.

These are the areas that are providing the rice, maize that feed us even though their lands may not be as fertile as the lands we have here. Our graduates know exactly what we are supposed to do but they go out there and the system is not ready to accept the new ways of doing things and then they say we don't learn enough, that is not true, I think we probably learn too much.

PART II — SCALE

CHAPTER 5

DIGITAL MARKETING FOR SMALL BUSINESSES

Princewill Omorogiuwa, Marketing consultant.

Princewill Omorogiuwa is the founder of Simon Page College of Marketing, a top-notch marketing training school, with branches in Ghana, Nairobi and Nigeria. Omorogiuwa worked previously in London training marketing professionals. While in the UK, Omorogiuwa was able to train about 3,000 students from 100 nationalities, most of whom eventually became high flyers in their different careers. He is an internationally-recognised marketing professional who fluidly combines digital marketing with traditional marketing to deliver measurable results whilst bringing openness, energy and leadership into all activities.

Princewill has excellent communication skills, supported by very strong project management, organisation and planning. He Initiates and develops excellent business relationships, as evidenced by repeat business offered. He sets high standards, thinks creatively, strategically and laterally to promote business development and to resolve issues. Brings global knowledge based on an interest in current affairs, brand relevance and international experience. He is a public speaker who is able to inspire and motivate and believes firmly in the future of a Digital Africa.

OPPORTUNITIES

The opportunities that technology presents to us in Africa especially for small and medium sized businesses are phenomenal. We are at a point in our history where we have the opportunity to communicate with millions of people without spending so much money. For those organizations who are not using technology as part of their marketing strategy, they are missing out on an obvious opportunity, and for those who are using it they can see significant improvement in their bottom lines and their ability to get in touch with a lot of people. So the numbers are good the numbers will continue to improve.

My response to people who have asked me in the past about some numbers when it comes to digital technologies and these are mainly people who will sit on the fence and say to you "how many people are online?" My response has always been that there are more people online today than there were last year. There are more people online today than they were two years ago and I can assure you there will be more people online next year than there are today.

I think that hopefully, people will no longer be asking those questions since the evidence itself is there. There are lots of organizations who collect data around the world who are actually tracking internet usage across Africa. The information on internet usage is available for people who doubt, hence we know that it is working. The big question of course is the impact of the increasing number of internet users on businesses and we will get to talk more about those later in this piece.

In marketing, the bottom line is about customers. You can talk about whatever technologies there are, you can talk about how exciting your products are but fundamentally all of these are meant to impact on a particular person and it all boils down to customers. So, unlike other disciplines, marketers have this idea that they are the ones who think about the customer all the time and their clarion call is to satisfy and to meet customers' needs and wants and of course like the accountants will tell them you meet those needs and wants profitably.

However, in today's business environment, you will find of course that it is not just marketing people whose sole responsibility it is to meet customer needs. You need the procurement people, finance, and critically today you need friends in technology and so together we work but we marketers are the custodians of the all-important customer satisfaction role. There is this notion albeit erroneous that you need a lot of budget to be effective with marketing, but it is not necessarily the case that in order for you to work, you need a lot of money. This erroneous notion exists because people still equate marketing to marketing communication, advertising etc.

Let's note that like any discipline there are first principles and components for marketing. We like to speak about the marketing mix elements and of this mix element there are seven very popular ones (and I like to say popular because some authors have tried to expand them beyond seven) and they are what we refer to as the seven Ps of marketing. One of those Ps is **PROMOTION.** Note that it is just one of them. But somehow because it is all catchy and all over on TV, radio and billboard that's all we tend to know about marketing. However, there is no amount of marketing communications that can compensate for a poorly designed offering.

So if the product or service doesn't work and it doesn't meet the need for which it was designed, it will fail hence the next element in the mix is **PRODUCT.** From an SME point of view where entrepreneurs are very passionate and very enthusiastic and want to change the face of the world, if you think about it, the product has to work, it has to do what it says it does and always note that it is credibility before visibility. The visibility part of it is all the marketing communications and truth be told, there are lots of companies who have succeeded without spending that kind of money. They have succeeded because they got the first principles right. They were able to make sure that their products met the needs of the customer and whoever they designed it for.

Now if you take out the promotion and the product you also have the **PRICING** part of it. You could choose whether out of ego you want to price your product through the roof or you want to price it to survive. You can also make the decision to price it to recoup all your investments within two weeks or you may want to play the long game and price it at a level that people can try the product and get to know whether this is something you want to keep on using long term, and then also there is the issue of accessibility which is where we must now talk about technology. For those people who have got products that can be digitized, the internet presents significant opportunities, huge opportunities. For those who have got physical products there are platforms that exist to help them reach more potential buyers such as jumia, olx, tonaton that you can use to distribute your items without carrying on huge fixed cost in terms of distribution vehicles.

There also is the **PEOPLE** element of the marketing mix. It is not the question of trying to find people who have got all kinds of fancy degrees. It is about finding people who buy into your vision and who believe in what it is that you are trying to do. Take time to hire people but please fire them quickly. Take time to hire because at the end of the day it doesn't matter how great your product or technology is, it boils down to people, then in as much as it is easy to say that people should develop products and make sure you have a big budget for marketing communications actually I say no.

Also, there is the **PLACE** and **PHYSICAL** evidence as part of the mix elements. For SMEs if they are in the services sector and if they provide a service then that becomes really important because people come into your premises to do business with you so at least the place should be clean. People who will meet them should be well presented, they should be presentable. For your online presence, you can look as big as you want.

The look and feel of your website must be impressive and these days you can build a powerful website with next to nothing and the websites are mobile responsive as well.

In addition there is the element of **PROCESS**. From the point where someone picks a phone and calls or submits an enquiry form at the website, and gets feedback must be well thought out. How does the process work? If someone buys your product and he/she doesn't like it or finds a fault and wants to return it and get their refund, for example, how does that work? So if you pay attention to each and every one of the above mentioned Ps you will be on the right path to getting your marketing right. The opportunity online is significant, not only are people able to use the online platforms to promote their business, but the internet in itself also provides opportunities inherently for people to exploit. There are different avenues to develop sustainable ventures, take for example mobile applications. Before these technologies, we had restaurants and hotels but because of the availability of technology tools, it has become easier to find restaurants and to find hotels.

Before these technologies we had car dealerships but now with platforms like cheki, carmudi etc you can now find cars to buy much more easily. However, there are businesses whose form did not even exist for example, Whatsapp and the various applications we now use on our phones. Today you will find someone in Ghana who developed an application that somebody can buy off as a business tomorrow for a billion dollars. Take *UBER* for example. People have gone on to develop games that have gone ahead to generate significant revenue for their organizations and what is interesting about these is the fact that these are not huge conglomerates of a thousand workers. People can still recall how much Facebook bought Instagram, how much money they paid for Whatsapp and these businesses didn't have many staff. If you look at the definition of an SME, all of these companies were SMEs.

In terms of the opportunities inherent in technology, Africans need to stop looking at the internet as just something they can use to go and do search or use to find people or to be connected to people. We need to begin to think about it differently that this is a fertile platform that can change the face of Africa because the next person that will come up with something that will be bigger than Facebook is on this continent and is probably not even yet plugged on to the internet yet.

In terms of opportunities, they are there for us, it is left with us to apply ourselves and our thinking so that we can exploit them and this perhaps is where we will speak to people who are responsible for curriculum in our senior high schools and also our universities. It is ludicrous that these technologies are not pervasive yet in the curriculum. I know one or two universities are driving the agenda for it but it should be pervasive. It should be as available in terms of education points as it is in learning the alphabets and that is only when our people can begin to think digital by default.

For the organizations that exist and want to use technology to drive their agenda forward, the opportunities are significant. Not only is it by far cheaper, but it is possible to reach one particular person and that is a tool for marketing people to customize marketing and offerings to reach the target individual. Never before have we been able to achieve that. All the money we spend on advertising and on billboards and radio and on TV, they do good work, no disrespect to them at all but to think that today it is possible for us to be by far more targeted, engaging and its possible for us today to track our conversion so that we know where to put money and where not to put money and not advertise to millions of people who do not even need, desire or want our products in the first place. Let me give you an example, we organized an event in Kenya, a master class for one of our program and that event was promoted only using social media and it was oversubscribed. The budget for that event was three dollars a day for the first week and we reduced it to two dollars a day for the second week and then one dollar a day.

In total we spent less than thirty dollars but the event was oversubscribed. It was very targeted so yes it is true that we need to do some marketing advertisements but it is not true that you need to break the bank or that you must be on TV. Having a website that can be found is very important and being able to educate people via your website using blog content, for example, is of great substance. These days, people can even use their mobile phones to record videos or what you might call vlogs that they can put online, so for SMEs there has never been a better time in our mercantile history for them to be successful.

We run a business which, if not for technology nobody would even know we exist. We work for businesses in Europe who found us because we have an optimized website, so when they searched for the services we deliver, their search query led to us. There is no way we could have run advertising on CNN or any of those international channels to gain their attention and this has enabled our country as a whole to earn foreign exchange because lots of people are being paid in Ghana by foreign companies simply because they found them online. I met a student who earns money through fiverr. She pays her school fees by providing content services online and she earns between five hundred dollars and one thousand dollars a month. When she graduates she might set up her own agency to provide content marketing services to clients from different parts of the world. This definitely is the time for Africa.

When it comes to the digital platforms, the first thing to look out for is the role you expect 'digital' to play within your entire marketing system. After you have clearly outlined the role you can then pick and choose which platforms you want to form that digital ecosystem for you. The first thing I will say is that your website is a hub of information about you and your business offerings so it is important that in the face of all of these fancy things, you don't ignore your website. When it comes to building the website, there are all kinds of platforms available and I am not saying this to give preference to a particular one. We have found from experience that, if you are building a normal website, wordpress gives you a lot of flexibility. I say that because just as there are more mobile applications on Appstore or Google play store than any other platform so is it with websites. People trying to build apps in Africa, for example, are encouraged to build applications for android enabled devices first before building the IOS version, whereas in Europe and the US, you find that application developers build for IOS first because it is the most popular operation system used. On building websites, you realize that wordpress seems to have the most plugins (i.e. apps for websites) so most people who are building plugins will develop for wordpress hence if you want your website to have all the features of a responsive site then you find out that wordpress will suffice.

When it comes to advertising, Google has a fantastic platform called adwords and it is great. Every other advertising service offered by any other platform seems to have taken its roots from adwords. If you learn how to use adwords for example, then it becomes easier to advertise on LinkedIn and Facebook and Twitter. So Google adword is the defacto platform when it comes to advertising online and it works and it does great work. Adword is easy to create, and the principle which is really clever is you pay per click.

For example; if someone searches for business books and the Small Business Bible's advert comes up, if the person does not act on it by clicking the link, you don't pay any money even though they've seen your ad. What that simply means is that you are paying for what you are getting: you pay when an action is initiated to visit the website link or initiate a purchase. This principle is very different from that of billboards or television adverts where you are paying for the eyeballs with no commensurate action or purchase.

In addition to that, you can also set your own budget so it's not a question of paying for a full page advert, the cost of which is predetermined to be six thousand Ghana cedis for instance. When it comes to online advertisement, you can set your budget for one dollar a day, twenty dollars, one hundred dollars etc. Take a look at the amount I am mentioning, these are monies that an SME can afford, hence if your budget is one hundred dollars per month you can decide to spend four dollars a day for twenty five days or different other combinations. On the other hand if you are thinking about marketing on radio, Television, billboard and other offline avenues then we will be talking about much larger amounts of money. So for people who want to advertise, adword is something that they should consider. And then of course, there is social media.

When it comes to social media, there are a plethora of platforms but the elephant in the room is Facebook. The reason why you advertise is that you want to reach a lot of people and there is no platform that reaches more people like Facebook does. It is prudent to have Facebook as part of your social media marketing strategy. If you intend to run only one social media campaign then you will have to think about Facebook first. That notwithstanding, I would like to reiterate that you need to know what role you want the campaign to play. In some situations you might find that LinkedIn might be more appropriate. For some of them, Twitter might be more appropriate whereas for many it might just be Facebook. Before you are able to setup an advertising campaign on Facebook, you need to set up a page as opposed to a profile which individuals have.

The profile is for individuals whereas the page is for businesses, organizations, brands etc. Whereas it is true that you can put up your content on a page and get people who follow you to see it, it is also possible to run adverts as well. It is necessary to run paid adverts because the fact that you have two hundred thousand fans/likes on your page does not mean that when you put up your content all of them will see it. In fact Facebook restricts what is referred to as organic reach. We once put up a post that reached two million people and that brings in the issue of the quality of the post itself. Lots of people shared it, why, because they found the content to be relevant. So across digital platforms you will hear the word "relevance". People's attention span is very limited so if your post is not relevant they won't engage with it but if it is very relevant and it resonates with them they will engage with it, they will leave comments, they will share it, they will like it, they will spread the word and that is why it is called social media. In simple terms what is considered relevant is what people want to consume. If it doesn't speak to me as an individual, if it doesn't resonate with who I am or how I see myself then, I will just move from it but if it resonates with me and I think my friends will like it then I share it. I agree with this then I like it or I have a different point of view so I will comment. All of these are engagements so whether it is positive or negative you have engaged with it and that is what relevance means. It is the difference between using the remote to either switch off the channel or stay with it. In this situation you chose to engage with it.

How do you measure the level of relevance of your post? Social media is equipped with a backend that provides analytics on how each post fared and you know numbers don't lie. If you put one type of content and you only got fifty people who clicked the like button, ten others who shared it, five comments compared to another type of content which got five thousand likes, two hundred comments and one thousand shares, these numbers should indicate to you the kind of content that resonates more with your audience. The good thing with digital adverts is that you measure the performance of each post in real time and you have the opportunity to continue making changes every single day to make your posts more relevant. The power is now in your hands unlike producing an advert for television where you probably go to master the shots in South Africa bring it back to Ghana put it on TV and if it doesn't work as expected there is nothing else you can do aside spending more money to produce a different ad.

When you put up a content on social media, spend some money like five dollars, four dollars or a dollar to promote the content and also monitor the feedback and see whether people like it or not. When it comes to using social media you have got to be mindful of the fact that people don't just want you to just sell to them all the time. You can't just have your product and keep on pushing it every single time because when you do that you send the wrong signal. People online want to believe that you care not only about yourself, hence you have to serve your followers before you sell to them.

This means you must give them content which they like, which even has nothing at all to do with your product or service. You must come across as being helpful by providing useful information that they can use for their everyday lives. When you then present information to them in a form of your products and services they are by far more receptive. People who only focus on selling their products do really badly on social media because people just push back and may even unlike your page because all you care about is yourself. When you think about it, if you are in a conversation with someone and all that the person does is to talk about himself/herself you don't want to be with that person next time. But when you are with someone who actively cares about you and is asking about your wellbeing and is giving you useful information to help you then you want to be around people like that all the time and that is exactly how social media works.

In training the youth to take full advantage of the information age, aside the usual content taught in schools we have to teach communication skills, emotional intelligence, and most importantly, students need to have digital skills. They need to be able to understand how online advertising works. They need to come face to face with the power of social media and also understand the role that websites play. They need to come to terms with the fact that communicating online is different from communicating offline. There are certain companies when you join them, they teach you to send professional emails because you need to understand the difference between communicating with someone you can't see and doing same with someone you can see. You also need to understand all the nonverbal skills that go with online communication and it is important these skills are taught in schools. Because policy makers in Africa were raised in a different age they do not recognize the power of technology. They are in effect robbing our entire society of the benefits that could have accrued to us as a result of exposure to digital technologies and people's ability to exploit it has never before been this easy. If for instance you think about what the entire GDP of some African countries compared to the amount Microsoft paid to purchase LinkedIn, you begin to understand the magnitude of opportunities the information age carries for Africans and how it can significantly change every aspect of our lives.

The question usually asked is can Africans claim the web and the information age to propel growth and prosperity among our people? My answer has always been that, I am not sure we can claim the earth any much as we can claim the web. However, as a platform, the web provides everyone with the equal opportunity to do as much as they can. The code that is used to write software in Ghana is the same code that will be used to write software in UK or anywhere else in the world. Technology is a global currency and we cannot talk about claiming it when we have not even exploited 0.001% of it yet. We have not even started internet of things, where different appliances in your home are speaking to each other. We don't even have operation systems in our vehicles yet but it is going to happen.

I am very pleased that lately I hear a lot about STEM- Science, Technology, Engineering and Mathematics, I am excited about it. Not that all of our lives must be subjected to science and technology but the fact that people are thinking and laying emphasis on it means that we can begin to educate our young ones properly. If we can teach kids in schools languages such as French, German and Mandarin, there is no reason why we cannot include coding as well because it is also a language. If we introduce them to it now by the time the kids are twenty years old, they shall have had twelve years of experience and they shall have done over ten thousand hours of coding and that is what will make them world class. Out of this we would find those of them who would be deeply passionate about technology and who will do things Bill Gate could only imagine in his dreams. That is where I think we ought to be heading towards.

CHAPTER 6

BRANDING FOR SMES, STARTUPS AND THEIR FOUNDERS

Bernard Kelvin Clive

"The personal branding guy who empowers others to live their dreams, brand themselves and publish books." Bernard is an Author, Speaker, and a Trainer. He is Ghana's foremost authority on Personal branding and Digital Publishing.

He is a Personal Branding Coach and Brand Strategist at BKC Consulting with over 10 years of experience in digital publishing. He has offered consulting services to hundreds of writers, poets, authors locally and internationally to self-publish their books. He is an Amazon bestselling author of over 30 published books. His ideas and perspective on branding is touted as unconventional and revolutionary and has won him many admirers including Seth Godin.

In January 2014, Springboard Virtual University named him as one of the 'Apostles of the New Economy' leading the revolution in digital publishing. He is the go-to-guy for digital publishing and personal branding.

He delivered the commencement address at the 46th congregation of the College of Art and Social Science at the Kwame Nkrumah University of Science and Technology. Perhaps the most quoted author and motivational speaker in Ghana. Clive is a passionate speaker on the subjects of "Personal Branding" and "Living Your Dreams": inspiring and empowering souls to achieve their God-given dreams".

BASICS OF BRANDING

When we talk about branding is it just the logo, a combination of colors or the name of a company? All of these entail what a brand is. However brands are really made in the minds of the market or the audience and basically the key word we use is "brands are perceptions". It's how people perceive you to be. How does the audience perceive Small Business Bible to be? It is for instance; the book that helps their businesses hence in their minds, it is all they think about when the name "Small Business Bible" comes up. So basically branding is how to manage people's perception. Per definition: I define branding as "the ability to constantly create a perception in the minds of your audience or your market that there is no product or service like yours by providing distinct value" and that is the thing that will set you apart from the other products in the market.

Most new businesses don't pay attention to branding. A few do, yet most of them throw in the words here and there without a deeper understanding of it, but those who pay attention to branding excel. This is as a result of several factors ranging from lack of understanding, financial constraints, lack of personnel to handle their branding activities. Most of them don't really know what branding is all about. They think it is about a logo, colors, slogans etc. However when they get the understanding and appreciate the benefits that go with branding a company, they begin to pay more attention and the return on investment is always greater and higher. Without that basic understanding of what branding is, throwing in a few words won't do much good. For startups to succeed in the business world with their products and services, it is essential for them to consciously create an identity that sticks in the mind of their market. This is what will give them the competitive edge to compete with bigger companies.

The first thing I tell SMEs is that, get a brand identity expert. Do not say because you are a startup you want to do everything yourself. When you get a brand identity expert he/she is going to design the logo, the colors, letterheads and it will not cost you that much, so that you focus on what you are good at. Most of the time we want to do everything on our own and that is one of the things that break SMEs. Invest a little in employing a brand identity expert to get your branding right. Then, you focus on whatever your business is and produce it well. Once your identity is done, you need to have a fair idea of what a logo needs to look like: what goes into a logo, what the tag line should be; but don't override the brand designer's work with your own personal feelings. You need to outsource that aspect and focus on developing your business.

It is perceived that, building a reputable brand costs a fortune. It may cost you in terms of time and effort because, nothing good happens overnight. There are two ways to look at everything, either you have the money to help you cut short the process or you invest a lot of time and energy to study and find your way out. So if you have money you can buy billboard ads, media ads, to get yourself known, but that is one aspect. After you have branded your product or service, when they come and taste what you have, is it what you said you have? That causes me to push in this popular bible passage. A story we all might have heard. It says "when the queen of Sheba heard of Solomon's wisdom and fame she went to see". So firstly they will hear about your business, they will hear about your new book, that's one channel through which people get to know about your brand; or they will see images on social media, offline billboards etc., and then they will come and experience and taste what it is that you are offering, to know if it is what you promised in your media campaign. If it is not, then your brand begins to fade away. People will see, they will hear, but they will want to come and taste and experience it, that is the brand.

In the process of building a brand, there are questions as to what should be done first. Let us take the waakye seller in your locality as an example. He/she probably has no signboard, no business card, no advertisement but people queue with big cars to buy the waakye. The question is why? The point is simply the waakye is good, it tastes good; so that is the value and once you have value, people will start searching for you and with that it helps you spread your brand easily. So the first thing I tell upcoming entrepreneurs, business owners and Small – Medium scale Enterprises is that, focus on producing distinct value and the rest can be done with ease. Once you have a very good product, irresistibly good product it becomes easier to market your product so, that is the first aspect of brand positioning, that's having a very good distinctive product/service.

One major challenge small – medium Scale enterprises face is the competition from multinationals and companies who have financial backing to out-muscle the small fishes in the market. The fact is, SMEs can't beat multinationals or huge companies who are offering similar products on the market. This is what I tell SMEs, focus on a niche market if you are currently serving the entire population. For instance, if I am producing a new soft drink and I brand my drink for only kids, then I can lower the price so that I am not targeting the same market these big multinationals are targeting. Also, still in the niche market, narrow your target down. For instance, I am going to sell my product to only schools, only churches or only mosques.

When you focus on a niche-specific market, you can easily either price your product a little bit higher or lower depending on what product you are selling. We know we have the big brands that are into the production of bags, belts and other products; yet you have seen a lot of African print bags and products in the market as well. This is what I tell young executives or entrepreneurs: instead of you trying to do African prints bags for everyone, why don't you focus on a small part of the market and say I'm doing African print bags only for kids. If a parent wants the same brand he wears for a kid your name, your product and your business will come to mind. Once you niche your product down you can then begin to extend into the market and then you look at how to expand, and that is the winning strategy against multinationals or big firms with whom you are competing in the market.

If you have a water company and you are looking to establish your brand in a market that has several players, you need to do a deeper research to know what your company is doing right and what you are doing wrong. Secondly, you would look at the audience and the market, who are we trying to reach with our new bottled water? If you are looking to reach the middle class or low income market, you should make sure it is affordable. When you find out these basics about your market, the next question is where do I get them? Maybe they are in schools, so you target the schools and you try to reach them through the headmasters or parents;

so you find out all these things. When these fundamentals are set in place, the rest becomes easy.

In designing any product, the first thing to critically think about is user experience. Always ask the question: who will use this product and how are they going to use it? Also make sure it is appealing to the eye because we want to see first. What is appealing to people is more likely to be bought than what is not. They need to smell, taste and touch, so appeal to the senses of people with your product design. These are the things to inform you in designing your product. Also, you look at the colors. I advise you to do a prototype so you get to understand how the customer relates to your product before you do mass production.

When you start a business, one thing you need the most is trust. Can the customer trust you to deliver as you have promised? In this age, if you cannot be trusted you have no business. The first quality asset you must build as an SME is the quality of trust. Make sure you are believable, trust-worthy and credible then you can push up your business with ease.

I also encourage companies to make their staff become their brand ambassadors. We encourage them to let their staff buy into the company's vision and mission. You need to create what I call a 'brand culture' for your company. You need certain rituals to let you bind with your staff. When the staff feel loved and cared for and don't feel like they are just exchanging their time for money, they are able to help in positioning their company's brand effectively whether online or offline.

The key thing is people buy into you the entrepreneur before they buy into your brand, and if they like you, they buy into your vision before anything else. So as a CEO, one thing you need to understand is that people will buy into you and your staff before they buy into your business. So if you treat your staff well, empower them and make them feel part of the company, your business will grow easily.

PERSONAL BRANDING

Who you are determines who gravitates towards you. If people do not know you or trust you they will definitely not do business with you; so how do you brand yourself to stand out in the market? The first thing that you need to do is to really focus on yourself. Though you want to reach out to others, you ought to be stronger in order to lift others up. It is said that to attract attractive people you need to be attractive yourself. So that if you want to reach the market you must position yourself properly because, like attracts like. In this age, people buy into people before products and services; so as an SME CEO and entrepreneur, you should know that people are buying into your vision, your brand, before they look at the product you want to sell to them.

The first thing you need to do in building your personal brand is ask your whys. It is very critical that you know your purpose in life and I don't mean about your business; I mean your personal mission statement. Your purpose in life is necessary because until you have a clear direction or purpose in your life, you will be building a fake brand. For every individual, you need to ask: why am I doing this and why am I here on earth? You need to delve really deep into your purpose. Once that is settled, you can then look at how to build your personal brand because I have seen a lot of fake celebrated brands who missed the mark of what God has called them to do. The fact that you can do something doesn't mean you are called to do it so as an SME CEO, know that what you want to do is what God has called you to do. Regardless of your faith or religion, what you are doing should resonate with your spiritual purpose on earth. Therefore, the foremost pillar in building your brand is **PURPOSE.**

In the word purpose, the first P is your Passion. What am I passionate about? Maybe you will like to see SMEs and entrepreneurs excel, you are passionate about entrepreneurship; so that is your passion, and your passion serves as your pointers to your purpose.

The next letter in purpose is the letter 'U'. The 'U' stands for - *UNDERSTAND* you. You need to really understand and understudy who you are. For instance, do you like black ties or red ties, why does a particular color appeal to you? You need to really understand yourself. And I tell people you need to date yourself. Take time for yourself and know who you are, that will help you position yourself properly in the kind of business you need to do, and then, you can thrive.

The next letter is 'R'. Find out what **RESOURSES** will help you position yourself properly. In this age we have books, podcasts, seminars, workshops and mentors. These are people and gatherings and products that serve as your resources. So you need to work hard on yourself because having a talent is just not good enough.

The next letter to consider in purpose is the other 'P' and that stands for **POSITIONING.** You should know what you are good at. If I can play a guitar, I can choose to play only acoustic guitars, that is called brand positioning.

Once you have positioned yourself very well, that will open doors to **OPPORTUNITIES** for you. This therefore represents the letter 'O'. For instance, for any opportunity that involves hosting a television program let's call Edem, for a good photographer let us call Kofi. Once your brand is well positioned opportunities will find you always.

The next letter to consider is 'S'. It represents the idea that in whatever we are doing as individuals or companies the aim of our existence is to **SERVE.** Small Business Bible is serving the community, serving SME CEOs, managers, and policy makers. Our goal as businesswomen and men is to serve; hence whatever your talent is, the ultimate purpose is to serve people without whom you will not be in business.

In the midst of all these, the last letter is 'E'; that is to **EARN.** When you do all the above you are going to earn trust, reputation and income. This is your purpose in building a brand. When you put all these things to use they are going to help you position your brand for corporate leverage.

Technology has several tools to assist us in branding and reaching our target audience easily. To reach a lot of entrepreneurs, to sell products or for employment of labor you need a social media platform called LinkedIn. You need to create a professional profile on LinkedIn because, that is where professionals are easily reached on the internet. Therefore, you choose the platform based on your audience and your market. If I am a photographer or I am in the food industry, one of the best platforms for me is Instagram or Facebook because people on these platforms want to see images and something appealing. Therefore, based on the business you want to do, you choose that platform. You can also use Pinterest, where there are a lot of images. If you want to be a writer then you can use plugin platforms like medium.

These avenues or social media platforms inform your decision based on what you are doing, what your market is and what you want to reach them for. Note that, without the social media platforms most businesses will not do so well. So, the first thing is to have a professional profile across board and be authentic. Don't fake your personality online because at the end of the day, the internet doesn't lie.

CHAPTER 7

TECHNOLOGY AS A CATALYST FOR GROWTH

**Derrydean Dadzie,
CEO Dreamoval**

Derrydean Dadzie is an accomplished Senior Executive who has achieved huge success across the banking, finance, health, agriculture, and technology industries. Leveraging extensive experience in digital business development and growth, he is a valuable asset for companies working to build new digital product offerings, improve user experience, increase customer engagement, or reduce customer churn. His broad areas of expertise include cognitive computing, big data analytics, mobile payments, organizational leadership, and digitalization.

Derrydean co-founded innovation and technology firm, DreamOval Limited in 2007. He took on the role of CEO at DreamOval Limited and has achieved tremendous success over the years as key contributor to numerous organizational achievements. He was responsible for building DreamOval's extensive institutional and bank - client network. Top-tier institutions and banks in Ghana and Africa such as GPHA, MPS, Standard Bank Group, GCB Bank, ADB Bank and Fidelity Bank utilize DreamOval's Enterprise and Fintech platforms to deliver innovative transactional services to their customers.

Dream Oval is doing quite a lot. We are exploring different geographical areas and we are also doing a lot about cloud innovations and we are adding more value to our payment platform.

Dream oval is a business that is made up of some of the most talented geniuses that you can find in our part of the world. We have a very young team and our core focus is to see how we can use technology to simplify life for businesses and for everyday people, hence we are consistently and constantly working towards finding new ways that we can employ our talent in technology to provide services that will simplify the way businesses operate and bring more value and profitability to businesses.

CHALLENGES FOR SMEs

Any SME out there will tell you that, the key challenge they face is money. Though there are other problems, money is the key problem every business faces. Sometimes it comes down to their ability reduce cost of production or their ability to let monies flow in as quickly as possible, so that they can always have money to run their operations. So, SMEs are having a very tough time trying to get access to the kind of money that they need and also they have a tough time getting the right technology to more or less bridge the gaps in their operations.

SMEs are facing problems regarding labor. Sometimes you don't have the kind of people with the skill set to enable you drive your agenda. We have issues around culture and I say we have that as a very big issue as it affects the way businesses are run. If you have an organization that does not have the kind of culture that will engender growth and profitability, and enhance the customer experience, we find that as a very big problem. In all of these we need systems, we need people, and hence we need to institutionalize some of the systems that are within the corporate environment.

SMEs have a basic problem around policy. The question is, do policy makers understand the kind of businesses that are running in the country? And are policies that are being enacted solving the problems that SMEs are facing? Is our tax policy solving problems that SMEs are facing?

About importation, are the policies solving the problems in that sphere? In this country we make huge imports from China so that, local supplies are competing with cheaper china-made supplies. How are we able to harmonize the level of need into the economy as well as the level of production? We are facing different challenges such as lack of desire to consume locally-manufactured goods. That is the Ghanaian attitude; where local goods are seen to be inferior and foreign ones are seen to be superior. There are myriads of challenges facing SMEs, and we have to find a way to fix them. And there are several of them, and we have to find a way to fix them.

We provide services for some banks that enable them to get their customers to be 'stickier'. This means we are providing them platforms that give them the capability to know their customers very well and provide them very bespoke tailored services that their customers can love and cause them to stick to the banks and make them more profitable. For SMEs, we have payment platforms and our cloud services which they can use. One of the key challenges we see businesses face is how to receive money, and we have been able to provide that capability known as "slydepay" for business. It is a platform that enables small businesses to pay their customers, service providers and suppliers and even pay salaries for their staff. It also allows them to receive payment from their customers. So we are more about the customer experience when it comes to platforms. We have our qikli platform that enables SMEs to reach out to their customers and tell them what is happening around their business, advise them, send them newsletters, and give them transaction notifications. All these things are done through technology-based channels.

TECHNOLOGY-BASED SOLUTIONS

One of the key things that businesses need to do is to understand their customers. In the banking sector it is termed 'KIC' that's "know your customer/client". To really get to know your clients, you need to have technology. Physically, you can interview them, fill forms about them and put it somewhere, but if you don't have the requisite technology, you can't make use of the data that you have acquired. For me what is important when it comes to technology is that SMEs employ technology to help them understand who their customers are, and that's something that I believe our software solutions such as enterprise Nurs help solve very well. Sometimes your data expire in the database but the company wouldn't know. Technology can actually help them inform their customers that "hey your driver's license has expired'. Technology helps us bridge the gap around customer knowledge. When it comes to issues relating to knowing your customer, the technology tools used mostly are the customer relations management tools (CRMs). There are CRMs that will help you run the whole trail from customer acquisition, through lead generation, to when you actually sell your product or service. There also exist post-sales customer management software.

We have technology that you can deploy that stays in your environment and we have technologies that you can subscribe to on the internet. Those are termed the cloud services and at Dream Oval we have technologies that will enable you do that. There are variant technology tools available for small businesses, however, the key thing about finding technology is to know exactly what you want. You have to buy technology from the point of your expected result, what result are you looking for? You don't employ technology because the next person is using it, you use technology because of your peculiar needs and based on the expected outcome. If as a business you can't really pinpoint what outcomes you are looking for, you might just have to sit back and then do those analyses. Audit your own systems and then determine which technology solves which problems.

Also, one key thing when it comes to technology is that you don't choose a one-size-fit-all-technology. You can actually have a specific technology to solve specific problems or deliver specific results, so if you are buying technology, you cannot say I want one technology which can do everything. There are softwares that are optimized for specific jobs and there is no problem with picking different software, and integrating them because in this day and age, we have technologies that even assist you to broker conversation between different systems and these things are there to actually help you. Software is there to help you make decisions so before you pick one, ask yourself what kind of decision do I have to make and what kind of data is required to help me make the best decision in the form of report or search? You should also look for efficiency.

Profitability is the chief goal of all businesses and employing the right technology can guarantee that a business will be profitable by cutting down cost and maximizing your gains. Let us take a simple business like a cold store. How do you tell if one freezer is up or not? You can employ technology that will tell you that "hey the freezer in this part of town is gone off or has a low temperature." How do you tell, for example, which branch of your business is doing well? You can employ technology". We are doing that for some of the banks, we have technology for them like the teller hub that will tell you which tellers are active and which tellers are not. Technology exposes all the nuances and the dynamics and little details in your business and by exposing them, it makes you optimize for more profitability and I believe that these things are very important in driving down cost and also improving growth and profitability in your business.

PAYMENT INFRASTRUCTURE

Now let us turn our attention to the payment systems. Payment is a big issue in Africa. The whole idea of PayPal, MasterCard and Visa haven't really caught on yet with the population. Recently mobile money is making lots of waves across Africa with billions grossed in transaction annually; but there are solutions that SMEs can take advantage of to streamline their payments and receipts.

When it comes to payment systems, we have different payment systems out there. Sometimes the exposed Ghanaians want an exact replica of what is happening in Europe or America in Ghana. One thing to note when it comes to deploying technology is to understand the people you are deploying the technology for. So many things can affect the deployment including their personalities, how the people behave, their culture, what their beliefs are, their everyday commute, what systems they are used to and their level of integrity. So many things affect why people use a particular technology. When it comes to payment, one of the key things I advocate for is to figure out how to calve a payment infrastructure, a flow or a system that fits the specific unique attributes of the people in a particular setting. So when you come to Ghana, for example we have a lot of banks and a lot of people use mobile phones. When I go to a bar how do I pay? Do I have to take cash out of my pocket and pay? Can I have access to my bank account? Can I use my phone to pay? In Ghana almost everybody has a mobile phone. We have realized that mobile money is really catching on. This is a platform that a lot of businesses can actually use.

For us what we believe is that payment should be ubiquitous and agnostic to challenges. That's why we have platforms like slydepay which enables you to pay from the phone irrespective of whatever channel or platform you are using. So, payment platforms for SMEs should enable the SME receive money from mobile money wallets, bank card and receive cash as well. However, that should be unified within a single payment framework that is linked to all the multiple payment infrastructure regulated by the central bank. If you come to a company this is how I see it flow: if you are a Human Resource company, for example, and you offer me service and you send an invoice to me, I should be able to be pay for it on the go. I don't need to sign a cheque and then send a courier service to send the check or send somebody to go and pay the money into a bank account. These are gaps that we need to close using technology. I believe that tech can actually flatten the payment flow and speed up cash flow for a lot of SMEs.

I will therefore entreat SMEs to adopt platforms that will enable them to bring in multiple payment channels but in one container. If you take a platform like slydepay; it enables you do exactly that. Payment should be done very seamlessly and entities and SMEs specifically should leverage on the payment platforms to pay for instance their workers. Let us take an SME that is into construction, for example, and has a lot of construction workers. If you are doing by the day's job and you are paying your workers by the day, you don't have to count money on the table and call them one by one to pay them. You can simply pick all their phone numbers, upload them unto a system and then by a click of a button they get their money on their phones. These are the kinds of payment systems and payment efficiency that we are looking for in our part of the world, and these technologies do exist. We only need to make use of them to enhance efficiency.

One thing that comes up whenever the mobile money payment system is discussed is the cost incurred by the companies that use the platform. There is a 1% charge on all mobile money transactions hence the sender needs to pay that transactional fee to avoid deduction at the receiving end of the transaction. This is seen as a nuisance by many SMEs who are always looking for ways to cut cost and maximize profit. The question I usually ask is: what is the cost of signing a checkbook? It's going to cost you not less than Ten Ghana cedis and when you sign the check, you are going to send someone to commute to the bank and that is also going to cost you transportation fare. In the case where you have a messenger who has a motorbike, that will cost you fuel.

There could be an accident on the way for which you will have to pay medical bills and you might also lose a life. By using mobile money, you are going to reduce the friction of movement and prevent the situation where somebody can bolt away with your money in the case of cash delivery and even in check transactions people can copy your signature and defraud you. There is fraud on the electronic platforms, but the volume of fraud is not comparable with what happens when money changes hands. Note that, with the electronic platforms, fraud can be checked and prevented through the proper security measures. So the electronic platforms sanitize the payment systems when it comes to business and you also get a detailed report on all your weekly/monthly transactions. In one way or the other, there is still a huge cost to be incurred when you use other platforms, which cannot be compared with mobile money.

As to why many small-medium scale enterprises are refusing to use available electronic platforms, I think it is just a matter of time. More people will rely on electronic payment due to the ease that comes with such transactions. Also we have a cash culture. People just love to see cash and as stated earlier, it is not easy to erode the nature of a people and their way of life, but with a lot of education and with a lot of work these gaps are going to be bridged overtime.

Sometimes the SME owners just don't have the time and they are not patient enough to sit down to study their systems to see how to improve them because, for some of them so far as there is cash they think that they are doing well, but when they employ technology they realize all the holes in their systems because the various electronic systems generate reports which you can study to know for instance where you are getting the most money from and where you are losing money the most. These are things that a lot of SME owners do not know, hence they wait until something big but negative hits them before they adopt new systems. However, I believe that over time these SME owners are going to integrate these platforms in their systems.

The other thing is that, the Ecosystem itself is still growing so we don't have a lot of people utilizing these platforms. If for example an SME gets about 10 customers coming to ask to use a specific digital payment instrument each day, the SME will be compelled to go and get this instrument. We have an ecosystem that is made up of less people asking to use electronic payments, hence we don't have the critical mass to compel the SMEs to actually come on board because nobody is asking them or pushing them for it. So these are some of the challenges. Also some SMEs are simply tech-averse and some of them are scared of what we call sakawa or 419 in this country – fraud. These dimensions have influence on the way payments are adopted across the world.

SYSTEMS

Let us now turn our attention to the macro level discussion. Technology doesn't happen in a vacuum. There are certain fundamental elements that need to be put in place for technology to thrive. In the new age, for tech to thrive, you need data; that means that internet cost should come down. So there should be a lot of money invested to make sure that cost of internet will comes down and I believe that we are reaching there gradually. In

2007 when we started our business, internet was so expensive but now internet cost has drastically reduced even though it can be better. We are getting better at it but we need to do more and we should incentivize the players in the data space and the internet space to put in a lot of infrastructure so that more people can be online. When people are online, they can educate themselves and businesses can actually do a lot more when people are online. Then, you don't have to travel abroad for meetings since some of the meetings that we attend can be held via video conferences. When people are online, even our judicial system can improve and there will be a lot more transparency and you can have interactions without being present.

When people are online we are going to reduce traffic jams because most of the things can be done in different remote locations. If people are online then they are not inclined to pick a car and travel to go for those meetings. When people are online we are going to have more vitality when it comes to life and yes, we are going to have the social media distractions but people are going to optimize the time they spend with people as well. When people are online you are going to get a lot more interaction, you are actually going to get a lot of feedback when you deploy or launch a product. So we need to really work around and fix our internet services. When we are not online we cannot do for example internet of things, we can't connect systems.

We also need to look at our transportation system. Currently, it's a hustle to go to work because we have too much traffic and sometimes it is really tiresome that by the time you get to work you are tired and demotivated. We need to put that infrastructure in place to enable people, parcels and cargo to move easily and I believe this is going to help SMEs a lot because people are going to come to work more focused. If we don't fix transportation we are going to still struggle when it comes to doing business, hence we need to start dreaming big when it comes to transportation, we need to start thinking about train systems and very smart ways of moving people around.

We need to put in place specific infrastructure that will drive manufacturing and production in our part of the world. These things concern me because without them we are consistently going to depend on outside manufacturing and that means that we are going to spend a lot more pushing money outside to bring things in for people to consume and I believe that these things are what we need to look at in different ways.

CHAPTER 8
WHY BUSINESSES FAIL OFTEN IN AFRICA

Captain Budu Koomson (rtd.), CEO Nexus Consulting

Captain Budu Koomson (rtd.) is an accomplished business executive with diverse experience and competencies both in Africa and Europe. He has over 20 years' experience in logistics, personnel management having served as the Head of Logistics Department and subsequently the Head of Personnel Department of Stockheim GMbH & Co KG at Dusseldorf International Airport (with oversight of four other airports) in Germany.

He joined UT Financial Services in 1999 as a Project Officer and rose through the ranks to the position of General Manager-Operations and Director of Operations in 2005, Chief Operations Officer in 2008 and finally as Group Chief Operations Officer of UT Holdings Ltd. in 2009. During his tenure as group COO, he was responsible for the International expansion and profitability of UT and successfully achieved this in three (3) countries outside Ghana by 2013, having established UT Germany in Hamburg, UT Nigeria in Lagos and the UT South Africa subsidiary in Johannesburg in 2011 amongst other achievements.

He had a short but adventurous career with the Ghana Army having served in roles as Presidential Guard commander, Adjutant 5th Infantry Battalion, Adjutant AFRC HQ, General Staff Officer – Intelligence (GSO III INT) 1 Bde HQ, served several tours of duty with the United Nations in the Middle East, and retired as a Captain in 1982. Captain (Rtd) Budu

Koomson is currently the Founder and CEO of Nexus Consulting Limited. He serves as the key consultant for Nexus clients in areas of Business, Financial Advisory and Training (especially to NBFIs and SMEs), Management and Leadership, Mentoring and Coaching, Strategy and Country Risk Analysis.

Captain (rtd.) is a fellow of IMANI Center for Policy and Education, an internationally acclaimed Think-tank in Ghana. Captain Koomson was appointed initially to the UT Financial Services' Board in 2006 and subsequently onto various boards in the Group and finally the UT Holdings Ltd. Board in 2009. He is currently a Director of Bentil Consulting limited and the Board Chairman of AJ Plant Pool Limited. He also sits on the boards of IMANI centre for Policy and Education and Axis Human Capital Limited. Captain is a motivational speaker and He also does public-speaking on mainly social issues among other topics.

When we talk of business, it is enterprise and I want to leave out the formal sector. In our part of the world (Africa), and in fact all over the world, the informal sector is very big. Even in China the informal sector and the SME sector is big. In Ghana according my research, about 80 percent of all business activities are in the informal sector. My experience on the ground is that about 90 percent of all business activities in Ghana are in the informal sector and most of them are in the Small – Medium Scale Enterprise (SME) sector. We have this hoopla about the oil industry. The oil industry is much regulated, highly technical, capital intensive, labor poor so it doesn't affect us much. If you take the government sector, well, it's formal and then we have the big multinationals that come with the formal structures so I will want us to orient our mind. When we are talking about businesses failing, let us talk about entrepreneurs in Ghana or in our part of the world and what causes them not to survive.

In my opinion the first cause of business failure is that, we have a preponderance of accidental entrepreneurs as opposed to deliberate entrepreneurs. I had the opportunity to live in Germany for a long time and running around the continent of Europe. What I learnt is that, business is a deliberate endeavor. People go to school and either you want to be a lecturer, an industrialist or you want to be an entrepreneur. If you want to get into business then you learn the process of it. Even for those who learn trades like medicine, if you want to set up your own hospital, you can't. You can't just go and open a shop that "I am a good doctor, I can cut everybody up and patch them up and so I want to open my own hospital. You will have to go to a school to learn the business aspect of your medicine or your trade. How do you hire right? How do you determine the size of your business? How do you prepare a business plan and how do you conduct your risk analysis? When you are done with the school, then you are given the permit to open your own business; otherwise you will stay in the government clinic or somebody will employ you. You can't become a businessman; you can't be a medical entrepreneur because you first have to learn the business aspect of your primary trade.

A lot of us in Africa get into business because three years after school we are still unemployed and on the streets. Then out of frustration, we enter into business, therefore it's accidental. Many of these business people are there by default, not by choice; and so if it is not by choice, then I presume you did not prepare well to get there. I have nothing to do so to survive, if I have some one thousand Ghana Cedis (GH¢1,000) then I can buy and sell. These are all accidental business people. Why do I say they are accidental? Because there is no plan and that is the biggest cause of the failure of businesses.

To be a businessman you have to be an entrepreneur and to be an entrepreneur let's explore what it means; "an entrepreneur is a person who organizes, owns or manages a business with considerable initiative and risk to make a profit", or "entrepreneurs are leaders willing to take risk with a huge amount of initiative, taking advantage of market opportunities and by plan to achieve what it is that he/she wants to achieve". If you are an accidental entrepreneur who landed in business, then you will never understand the risk in business because you just have to survive. Unlike the one in Europe who has gone to school and has prepared and knows the risks associated with the business.

Secondly where is the initiative? It was not a deliberate thing like; "oh I have spotted this opportunity and I want to exploit it". The accidental entrepreneur is broke so if he can get an uncle somewhere to give him some money he starts to buy and sell. What was the plan? His only initiative here is survival. There, it is desperation and that is what I call the accidental entrepreneur. If by divine providence this venture succeeds, he/she is succeeding but you see the old man upstairs is not always looking at everybody. Sometimes I think he goes for a nap and on your watch the old man may be sleeping and you will get into trouble. We have a lot of accident people, so once you are accidental there is no process.

I always tell business people who come to borrow money from us or when I do this business incubation or entrepreneurship training, I tell them, business is a process; you have to think systematically through the problem or the opportunity to mitigate the risk to get the profit or the benefit. However, if you say process, the accidental entrepreneur didn't start the business deliberately; he/she got there by accident so it's not eureka: big idea. So we say, the business idea must be crystal clear in your mind as to what you want to do. Once you put it in your mind, normally we say have a dream; you have to dream the success. With this accidental guy who is desperate where is the success being dreamt? You have to visualize the success and that will spur you on so you have that desire to achieve that aim.

Now this guy who is desperate, if it means selling banana he will sell it, if it means selling maize he will sell it, if it means being a vulcanizer he will do it. Whatever that will keep body and soul going he will do it, hence he is not even focused as to the dream or the desire. Once you have the burning desire to be an entrepreneur, you need to have the idea and have sharp focus, and once you do, you have to will it. You have to be able to visualize that success, that particular business that you want to create, the empire that you want to build. After that you have to nurture it. In the book think and grow rich Napoleon Hill says that "desire is the beginning of success". He continues to say that "the starting point of all achievements, the first step to riches is the burning desire to be and to do that which you dream about" and that is the starting point. Dreams are not born out of indifference, laziness or lack of ambition. If we say businesses are failing we need to know how they started.

SKILLS ACQUISITION

Once we have an entrepreneur, hopefully he/she is not an accidental businessman/woman but, even if you are an accidental entrepreneur you can learn the process. So you have to define your vision and be crystal clear. What is it that you want to be and what is it that you want to do? Now if I want to be a pilot then I must know who I am. If I'm afraid of height and I want to be a pilot, is that possible? You want to be a seaman yet you fear water, you want to be a pastor yet you can't keep your libido down, you know you are a thief yet you want to be the Pope. You have to know yourself. We call that self-awareness. Some people are not suited for certain jobs; so if you know you can't keep your hands in your pocket and you have long fingers don't be a treasurer to something. What are your strengths and weaknesses? You alone know yourself best If you want to do a certain business, you have to acquire the relevant academic knowledge. If you want to be a businessman you must know your profit and loss. You want to know what a business plan looks like and entails; the academic qualification is very essential.

If you want to be a blacksmith, there is a technical school for it. If you want to do business, there is a school to teach business and you must build the capacity to succeed. We usually hear stories of successful entrepreneurs who dropped out of school and today they are multi billionaires. There are some who never went to school and yet are succeeding as entrepreneurs and we are told you don't need education and that all you need is to get the desire to start your own business; but this narrative is a big fallacy. For the examples that are cited, do you know the millions of businesses that collapsed and died because those entrepreneurs lacked the requisite skills? For every successful football star there are thousands of aspiring football stars who got brokenhearted and died. There are billions of people on this planet but how many Zuckerbergs can we show; how many Bill Gates can we show?

Even with these people they had the desire to do something and they didn't go there out of hunger. Most of them were in the best schools in the world: the Harvards, Stanfords etc. They only got bored with systems so let's be careful about that one. I wouldn't want people to go on faith, let's go by plan. It is the typical Ghanaian/African thing; we are always looking for the breakthrough. Instead of doing hard work we are looking for shortcuts to success. It won't work so therefore you have to get the process right. If you want to be a pilot get the requisite skills; you want to be a Pastor, go to a Bible school.

Formerly, there used to be the apprenticeship system, where you will be an apprentice to somebody till you are well prepared to be on your own. But these days because of desperation, you finish school and you think because you got your one thousand (1000) or three thousand (3000) Ghana Cedis, you want to do business with no apprenticeship. I remember once I was in my office when a hungry looking young man came into my office. It was about 2 o'clock in the afternoon. He was all sweaty and pretty aggressive. He used to be a student leader in one of the leading Universities in Ghana.

In addition to that, he was a National Union of Ghana Students (NUGS) executive and he was an A1 student. After school he had a business plan in his hands and he was looking for someone to fund his project. I asked him: how much is the project? He said it will cost a total of thirty five millions dollars ($35,000,000). It was a very technical thing, a TV station for the whole of West Africa. He ranted and said for three years nobody was minding him and people don't want to fund new businesses and we are not helping the young people. I said: young man sit down. Are you certain this business is what you want to do? He said yes. I asked him, have you worked in any radio or TV station before? He said no. Have you employed one human being before? He said no but he was working with other people. I said have you trained somebody before? He said no. Have you prepared a duty roster for people before? He said no. So I asked him: how are you going to run your business? Then I gave him the story of Komla Dumor who wanted to get into broadcasting so badly that when he got to Joy FM, and for the first year he was sitting behind a motorbike distributing leaflets in traffic. He didn't get in there straight into the TV room or the news room. But by the time he got into the newsroom he had built his apprenticeship. He had worked at the foot of somebody and he had gone through the mill so when he hit the international scene, he exploded.

He had a dream, he prepared for it, he worked hard for it, he willed it into a desire and he was aware of himself, he knew his strengths. Also, there is the issue of reality check. Are you sure that this business that you want to do is really what you want to do and are you cut out for that business or it's just for survival? Because some of us are good at being number 2 or 3 men, but when you are at the forefront where your yes or no pushes things, a lot of people chicken out. You need courage, are you sure you want to shoulder that responsibility? Some people have a very bad sense of reality check in the sense that, they see the facts on the ground but they wish it were different and so they live in dreamland, but the facts on the ground are the facts on the ground.

SELF MANAGEMENT

Self-management is the next salient factor in self-development. If you are lazy, you will not succeed as a businessman. It takes a lot of self-sacrifice and self-discipline, hence you have to be able to manage yourself. Eschew immediate gratification and blowing the money. Rather save and invest instead of building with the few thousands that you have got. Also, you have to be able to manage your emotions. Sometimes you don't even want to do something but you have to do it. Then you will have to be socially aware. Where am I? Is the environment right for my business? What is defined as wrong, what is acceptable and what is not acceptable in this environment? Business is about people, so learn the skill of relationship building. There are some people who can tell you: give me anything and I can sell it. That is because they have a way of connecting with people, they have a way of selling and they have a way of presentation.

You are doing the business so that somebody will come and buy your product or service; and if you don't know how to build relationships, how do you survive? There are so many businesses I have seen collapse because the owner fell ill. The business is still there, the products are still there but if people come looking for Maame Serwah and she is not there, they leave and say I will come later when Maame Serwah returns. This is because Maame Serwah has built this rapport with the people, or someone has even heard of this Maame Serwah and has come to see her. We should be able to build relationships. You also have to learn to manage your staff. To be successful you have to use other human beings and if you can't manage them, how do you succeed? Manage your staff, manage your customers, and manage your creditors. You have to be able to manage relationships to be a successful entrepreneur.

THE CULTURE DEBATE

There is the assertion that our culture hinders our ability as Ghanaians/Africans to be business savvy. I will say yes and no. I can't say yes it's our culture; because our fathers were successful businessmen. They never went to school yet they were successful cocoa farmers, fish traders, salt traders etc.; so I wouldn't place too much blame on culture though culture has a big content in there. We rely on people such as uncles etc. to inherit their fortune; hence we tend to be lazy. Also, when your business succeeds, culture then comes in where you are supposed to take care of people: your nephews and your family and friends will be expecting jobs and if you don't employ them then you are tagged a bad person. Also at every funeral you are nominated as the chairman and expected to contribute so much. So culture plays a part, but, if you went through the process and had a plan you can mitigate it. This is why I say it is very important to plan because in the plan you would have been taught in business school that, you recruit on merit but not based not on relationships. That notwithstanding, if you recruit relatives, you could train them. In as much as culture plays a part, I will say you can plan against the cultural risk because we have businesses that are succeeding. They are in Ghana and they are in the same cultural pot. So culture plays a part but I think we are blaming culture way too much for our own failures and I believe you can mitigate the cultural risk.

EDUCATIONAL SYSTEM

I have said repeatedly that we have to seriously look at our educational system. In our educational system we have looked mostly at the IQ - the academics. But the EQ - the emotional intelligence, the person himself, the intrinsic person, his values, his character and who he is, is mostly ignored. Emotional intelligence is now proving to be more important to success than academic capacities. If both of us were BSc. holders and we got into business, why will one succeed more than the other? It is the intrinsic you that comes into play because all things being equal one will succeed more than the other. What accounts for this is who this person is, the soft skills that the person has, the way he relates to people and how he manages his own emotions and himself. Emotional intelligence carries a whole weight on its own, so, it's not always about the IQ and education. Education is important, but we also have our Kwahu businessmen who are not so educated but are succeeding. So I will say that yes, education is important but we are not putting enough emphasis on emotional intelligence – the soft skills that will make you succeed as a businessperson.

Also, we are neglecting entrepreneurship. We churn out a lot of graduates every year into the market-place but how many jobs are there? These graduates have however learnt something so, why don't we teach them survival skills in addition to what they have learnt instead of just giving them the theory? We have students who have gone to Institutes of Professional Studies or the Technical schools, finished and got the skills but for three years they will be looking for a job, why? Because he/she was not taught about how to translate this skill into success or a source of livelihood. We don't teach them the entrepreneurial aspect of what they are studying. There was this young lady, a relative about whom I was told "oh she is very intelligent". She did her masters in biochemistry, and then came to us looking for a job in a financial institution. I asked, what are the business opportunities in biochemistry? You should be looking at the factories like Uniliver and all those people producing foods. Someone should have told her the business potentials in learning biochemistry. By doing that, she would have been given the entrepreneurial and survival skills to survive outside somebody's office; and that is what is failing in this part of the world. I believe the major reason why we are not able to equip our graduates with survival skills is the lack of planning, because it is somebody who develops the curricula and there is clearly a disjoint.

I have been in industry for a long time and I am still hanging around training people. You see that the graduates who come looking for jobs have the raw knowledge but you realize there is something missing. You get a Master of Business Administration (MBA) student come to your office, if you ask him/her to process a loan for a client, listen to the person and interrogate the loan applicant, he/she gets stuck. He/she does not know where to start from. He/she doesn't even know what questions to ask because he/she has been taught business planning, cash flow and other theoretical stuff. If you go to Mokola there is no business plan, there is no cash flow but you have an MBA, you should be able to process a loan for the guy in Agbogbloshie selling maize or chicken in the market, but we don't teach them these things. So we have to teach the entrepreneurial skills on all levels so that if you don't get a job you can survive. Because there is no entrepreneurial training, graduates come out and they are perplexed. They come out and they think that society owes them a job or a living society owes them a living and that is one of the biggest gaps in our educational system, they were not taught entrepreneurship or survival skills.

We need to inculcate practical entrepreneurship relevant to each subject of study. If you are studying engineering, what are the entrepreneurship opportunities in that field? Engineering entrepreneurship is different from medical entrepreneurship. There are the general entrepreneurial skills, but if you did biochemistry what can you use that to do? What types of businesses exist and how can you go about building one? When we say entrepreneurship it must be entrepreneurship tailored to one's area of study.

The argument that educational institutions have a duty to train students to be able to think and to analyze things critically and not to necessarily prepare them for a particular job in my opinion does not hold water. The question I ask repeatedly is why am I going to school? Is it just to think? When I get workers in my company I ask them this question: why did you go to school? At the end of the day, it is to take care of body and soul, otherwise we are producing graduates who will not survive outside their fathers' houses. I am learning and studying to take care of body and soul - to survive otherwise we are wrong. That is why I said we have to look at the curricula and all these things very critically. We have to subject these things to analysis so it's a big one we would want to find out from the educationists. Why are they educating these people?

Just to think critically? To do what, to go to space or to survive? They are growing up, they will get a family and corresponding responsibilities so they are being educated to be able to get body and soul together, to be comfortable as a human being and to contribute their quota to society. So if I can think but I can't work and what I am thinking about won't bring me anything then where are we going? Why do we even have all this hoopla about politics? When politicians are canvassing for votes they all come in and they say that if you elect us we will make sure that your welfare is improved.

They are educated but they don't go about saying when you elect me I can think. It is all about your welfare, it's about your wellbeing, your survival wherever you are. If the main premise of our educators is to make people argumentative, to be able to think but we don't know in what direction they think, then I think we have a big problem. I am not an education professor but I am telling them I am in business and we have a big problem.

RELEVANT SKILLS FOR SUCCESS

I have been involved in the training of several workers, and the first thing any company needs to do is to ascertain the traits they would want their staff to possess to ensure the survival of their company. This is because most of the employees are going to come to the firm right after school and all they bring with them is the theory they have accumulated in school. What will make the difference in the life of your company? Also, we often neglect the aspect of assessing the personalities of the people we employ to work in our companies. You must ask questions like who is this person?

Every company should have values, at least three values that define who you are as a company. The values dictate how you behave towards customers, inspectors and other stakeholders. If we say, 'respect' is one of our values, we must respect ourselves and others. If we say, 'truthfulness' is our cardinal value, we should mean it and define it and live it. Hence, that becomes the character of the company. Therefore these values should be the underlying factor in assessing who will fit in our organizational culture and who won't.

In "O" Level, we were taught factors of production to be land, labor, capital and entrepreneurship. Among these, the most important factor of production is labor, so you have to pay attention to the character and the make of these beings you are employing. The first thing is the character of this human being. If the character is right, a lot of things are solved. You cut away laziness, lateness, you tell them that you want speed, and things like truthfulness should become a part of your culture. When you lie, you are sacked. Punctuality means punctuality. When we want reports on a project, nobody should ever dream of giving an excuse as to why he/she didn't finish. Before you can be successful, you need to have a set of values that identify the way you behave as an institution.

Recruitment is a crucial aspect of the success of any business venture, hence I always say, "Recruit right". If you recruit wrongly you have a bigger problem. So first and foremost, you want to know what competencies you are looking for and then you also want to find out what makes the person tick and where the person's interest lies. There are questions that will illicit those answers; especially what excites the person. What are his/her life expectations for himself? Some people have no ambition so when they come into your company they are not going to contribute anything. I have to see a burning desire in your stomach to be somebody in order to employ you. You ask an interviewee sitting in front of you where they would want to be in five (5) years and he/she starts looking around like somebody is asking a different question. Such a person is really not going anywhere. There are other questions you can pose to find out whether the person has good ethics. For instance: if something is wrong, but somebody begs you to do it, will you do it out of pity? If he says "yeah maybe" then you are in trouble. You have to try to recruit right.

The questions you will pose should illicit both the academic and the soft side of the person. What is his character like? Some people are fatalistic, some are pessimistic others are optimistic. Is he/she an entrepreneur or only a worker? Some of these companies out there such as Apple are not only being powered by the CEO. They get workers who are thinking like entrepreneurs, hence they are working in the business as if it were theirs.

I remember when I joined UT it was just one year old. One Saturday I sat down and I drew up a plan titled "UT international". We had only one branch and I had divided the whole world into regions. Ghana was one region, West Africa was one region, and Southern Africa was another. London was one region (that is Britain) and Europe was the last. All my colleagues laughed. Seven to eight years later, I will get into a plane and tell the CEO - Kofi Amoabeng that I will have to go and visit our branch at Hamburg. I come back after two weeks and say: oh I have to go to Johannesburg, the next time I say I have to go to Tamale to visit our business. You will have workers who will push your business for you. It is not always going to come from you as the business owner or entrepreneur. You have to find out what is making this person tick, what excites his passion, if I give him the chance will he go far or he will sit there for me to come back to meet him where he is sitting. You have to be critically careful about the type of people you recruit. Recruit for the right competencies and the right academic qualifications, but it comes down to the human being. I always say it comes down to the human being because it is he/she that makes the difference.

UT Financial Services was all about lending and fast crude lending because, we were lending to the SMEs and we were collecting our money actually better than the banks who were giving to big companies. When I looked at our employees, the best performing credit managers didn't study finance in University. One did English, the other did Spanish and one did Industrial Arts. So it's about "who am I hiring, and what is his makeup?" You need somebody who is prepared to work. If we can teach monkeys to dance why can't we teach a human being to do something? The basic qualifications are necessary because you cannot do anything without them but beyond that, look at the innate person.

Then you also have to know the portion of the market you are in. For instance if you are going to lend to somebody whose address you can't locate on the map, what do you do? You want to lend to somebody in the construction industry meanwhile the government hasn't paid the contractors for three years, what shows that yours will be paid in six months?

You have to know your clients and you have to know the industry you are operating within, these are the things I will teach my staff. Know your business, the characteristics of your business. If somebody brought you a business proposal you should know if it is a recurrent business or a continuing business. Is it a close circuit business? How do I analyze this type of business? If somebody comes to you that he/she has a school and wants to borrow money to do expansion works, will you lend that money to him/her? Will you lend it to him at the first term, second term or third term? This is the training I recommend for staff.

Several financial institutions lend money to people and firms alike but majority of these money lending companies do not succeed and fold up because of big loan defaults. This is because the people doing the analysis to lend the money really do not understand the industry and the SMEs. At NEXUS I tell my staff to understand their market and who they are lending to. What is the character of the SME you want to give money to? Know the environment within which they are operating, if you know these basic elements about 70% of your risk is cut out. Therefore when you are doing your analysis you should always be alert.

MOTIVATION FOR EMPLOYEES

I think the first thing you want to know is the people you are working with. Who are these people? Then you build on their weaknesses. Don't try to catch them on their weaknesses because it is a chain link, and the chain is as strong as its weakest link so why would I want to catch you on your weakness! If I realize your weaknesses I will give you tasks that will avoid your weaknesses and rather explore your strength whiles working on your weaknesses, so first get to know your people inside out.

Secondly, treat them like you want them to treat you - respect them. Don't take yourself too seriously, don't think you should have all the answers or you should be the most intelligent person in the room. Sometimes even if you have the answer, solicit answers from them, let them feel that they are also appreciated as having something in their heads. Make them feel that they can also contribute to the company, get them involved. I have dealt especially with small teams and it is more difficult to manage a small team than a big team because, if there are five people in your team, each one is 20 %. If one is down you are in trouble; unlike if they were a hundred. So your senses should be sharper on the individual than their training. Also, give them responsibilities and then do a follow-up and offer to help if they ask for your help. Let them know that you will come and check, let them know that you are interested in their development as people.

SYSTEMS

For SME businesses to succeed I would say we need better legal systems

because resolving business dispute through the court system is tough. We need an enabling environment. Even registering properties and checking on collaterals is very difficult, so the legal framework should be strong.
We need business incubators. We don't have many of them but I am actually surprised we have a few of them around. They are not popular and people don't know about them. We have the Ghana Centre for Entrepreneurship Development and Innovation. It has been in existence since 2011.

They grow businesses and they have a database of job vacancies, institutions, business opportunities and matching opportunities etc. Then there is the Business Supports in Ghana. They also have a database and help small businesses through business planning, nurturing them for export readiness. Then we have the Africa Investment Management Services Limited, which was formed in 1994, focusing on assisting medium size businesses. There is the Association of Ghana Industries (AGI) formed in 1958. There is Busy Internet's Busy Incubator program. We have EMPRETEC which focuses on capacity building. There is Good Morning Africa, (GMA) which is in existence in Ghana, Rwanda and South Africa. They organize to eliminate the impediments to businesses in the SME sector.

We have the IntEnt and the Ghana IntEnt Business Club, a Dutch NGO which has helped to form 60 businesses that are operating in Ghana. We have the National Board for Small Scale Industries (NBSSI) which has business advisory centres in 110 districts across Ghana. They provide capacity, financial, technical and managerial assistance to micro companies and businesses, so you need business incubators. We need also to make sure that institutions like (GIPC) Ghana Investment Promotion Centre are functioning effectively, EXIM bank should popularize what it does and make it easier for people to access these things. The National Investment Bank (NIB) should be a place where businesses can go for cheaper monies and the conditionality to get the loans should not be 5 years' experience. Agricultural Development Bank should perform its core function. They now operate a universal banking license so the agricultural sector will not be their major area, but people are crying for Agriculture loans. I did some agricultural based loans and they all failed because I did not have the agricultural technical knowledge. I could only sell money. If the Agricultural Development Bank could have some agronomists who will know the cycle and the risk in the sector, that will help.

WINNING

Let's look at the issue of us not being able to build transgenerational companies. In other places, people build companies and they die and they pass it on to other people. There are companies that have lasted for hundreds of years, but in our part of the world we don't see these things. It is simply because there was no plan. "Papa Kwasi Manu gets into a type of business because his father is into it. The business is succeeding and when father dies, son takes over. It has to be deliberate, it has to be strategic, and how many businesses have strategic plans? So one year, two years after the death of the primary person the thing is dead because there was no plan to carry it on through the generational periods. There has to be a plan, what exactly do you want to do, what do you want to build? Do you want a permanent structure or something that you will die with? It is very often not discussed and it doesn't even strike our business owners that, as your company is growing, you have to put proper structures in place. You would want to now have the sales department, the marketing department and the administrative department. It has to be in the plan and you have to have a strategic plan. Where do you want to take this business? Now if you have a plan as to where you want to take this business and people know the plan, you will die, they will suffer a little but the business will survive. Do not be an accidental entrepreneur; be a deliberate guy, take charge of your life or something or someone will take charge of it for you. Plan your life; know what you want to do, know where you want to go. Plan to get there and get excited about the journey, count your little blessings, because as you are able to chalk the little successes, it encourages you for the next step. Finally, you should know what your success will look like when it finally arrives.

www.ingramcontent.com/pod-product-compliance
Lightning Source LLC
Chambersburg PA
CBHW030442220526
45464CB00006B/2386